IRREVERENT,
IRREPRESSIBLE,
IRRESISTIBLY
IRONIC

The Fine Art of Advertising

BARRY HOFFMAN

STEWART, TABORI & CHANG
NEW YORK

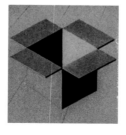

Table of Content

Aristocrats, actresses,
Cosimo de'Medici, Pope Juliu

mal fat. **He's tall . He's sexy.** Sex Sells. **No one has her reputation.** Surreal.
d Walter Paepcke. Democratic-commercial-vulgar-kitschy-campy flux.
s powerful fusion of art and advertising. Was this a further degeneration into

Americans are often described as a people with short attention spans and no memory for history. Henry Ford took a lot of flack for saying "History is bunk," but the full quotation is something that a lot of Americans would easily agree with. "History," he said in 1916, "is more or less bunk. It's tradition. We don't want tradition. We want to live in the present. And the only history that is worth a tinker's damn is the history we make today."

This rings true in America because we were always billed as the "new" world. We are the country that creates new ideas and produces new things. What came before isn't merely a tradition, a heritage, or a foundation; if it isn't new it isn't at the heart of being American.

America is the product of European imaginations; its government was structured on the precepts of eighteenth-century rationalism. Out of the Age of Reason came a country whose origin wasn't rooted primarily in tribalism, ethnicity, or territoriality. It was rooted in a point of view. No other country had ever introduced itself to the community of nations with so succinct, evocative, and inspiring a phrase as the one that became America's calling card.

"Life, liberty, and the pursuit of happiness" is more than just a few fine words. It is the idea that drives and defines the American experiment. We are used to seeing those words in contexts that are historical, political, and philosophical, but this is a book about advertising and fine art. Seen through the lens of advertising, "life, liberty, and the pursuit of happiness" reads like a brilliant tag line, a pithy slogan that positions the brand essence of America.

Indeed, the proverbial "big idea" of America is not to promise happiness. It is rather to promise enough justice and enough order to allow for enough liberty so that you, and

everyone else, can *pursue* happiness. Liberty remains the North Star of America's idea of itself in our political culture. The arguments we have with each other about freedom of speech, privacy, and the other protections of the Bill of Rights are not very different from the arguments Madison and Hamilton had in the *Federalist Papers*.

But the evolution of the pursuit of happiness is a whole other matter. If liberty is our guiding idea in the political realm, then pursuit of happiness is our guiding idea in the social realm, the realm of personal psychology and national culture. While Madison, Jefferson, and Hamilton had imaginations prodigious enough to create a form of constitutional government that could endure for more than two centuries, none of them could have begun to imagine the world we live in today.

In fact, most people who grew up in the last fifty years find it hard to get a clear fix on what's old and what's new. It feels like the only thing that is constant is the ever-increasing rate of change. Fads, fashions, trends, and movements blow through our days like wind through an unstable weather system. Lines that were etched in stone become lines drawn in the sand. Notions of status and fixed distinctions between highbrow art and its lowbrow cousins dissolve before we notice they are gone.

Above: A society organized to pursue happiness also generates a lot of anxiety. Edvard Munch's *The Scream* has become the poster child for all advertisers who want to show they have empathy with those feelings.
Opposite: Washington isn't just crossing the Delaware in Eastman Johnson's copy of Emanuel Leutze's famous canvas. His patriotic troops are also saving their valuable electronic treasures while defending our future right to pursue and protect the stuff that happiness is made of.

A DECLARATION of INDEPENDENCE *for your* STUFF.

▣ Now you can COMBINE your house, your laptop, your sport-utility vehicle, your cell phone, your bass boat--and more--under one UNIQUE insurance policy.

The ENCOMPASS Universal Security Policy. Declare your INDEPENDENCE from the inconvenience of separate policies. ASK your Independent Agent today. For the agent nearest you, CALL toll-free 1-866-760-6050 or visit encompassinsurance.com/34.

ENCOMPASS.
INSURANCE

LIBERTY, JUSTICE, AND REALLY GOOD INSURANCE.

We live in a world where boundaries are fluid and where things that were once serious are all too easily made trivial. If thinking about "life, liberty, and the pursuit of happiness" as America's tag line makes you more than a little uncomfortable (it is, after all, a profoundly revolutionary idea whereas advertising is aggrandizing, commercial, and meretricious), then you're not alone. There is an inherent tension between the high democratic ideals of America and our penchant to define everything in terms of the marketplace.

In the hierarchy of cultural criticism the lines drawn between art and advertising started out fairly clear. Art is high. Advertising is low. Art is elite and refined. Advertising is vulgar and democratic. Art is original. Advertising is derivative. Art is a product created by people to express their personal vision. Advertising is created by people who get paid to sell a product. Art is defined by the truth of the insight it expresses. Advertising expresses the insight of truisms. Art is disturbingly honest. Advertising is only as honest as it has to be, and occasionally less. Art is eternal. Advertising is ephemeral.

One does not solve the world's problems over a glass of white wine.

Dewar's

The rise of our consumer society has made it increasingly difficult to keep those distinctions clear. This book will take a new look at the cultural space where fine art and advertising meet. It is neither a history nor even a comprehensive survey; that volume would be ten times larger. It is an exploration into that space where serious stuff from the Old World of European art and from the New World of American art is cunningly, irreverently, and ironically put to work doing the one thing that Americans who take advantage of their liberty to pursue their happiness do best: selling.

The overwhelming growth of consumer culture has many sources. It was certainly fueled by the national determination to pursue happiness. While religion, politics, ethnicity, and regionalism tended to divide us, we all participated alike in the culture of selling. It is one part of our society that is truly egalitarian. As the technologies of communication, image reproduction, and distribution became more sophisticated, advertising became the most prevalent form of community.

Above: Rodin's *Thinker* is one artwork that advertising has turned into a solid gold cliché. The irony is that reproductions of high-culture images reach more people more often through advertising than through any other medium.

There is no end to the ambivalence we feel about advertising. On the one hand, we like it. How often have you heard that the most interesting things on TV are the commercials themselves? Indeed, after the Super Bowl or the Olympics or the Oscars—events famous for their sizeable national audiences—*USA Today*'s polls rank the favorite ads, as if the events were merely vehicles for the real competition between the sponsors. Adcritic.com, the iconoclastic Web site, was so successful, it had to stop operation. Like many dot-com ventures, it couldn't figure out how to make money letting people see all the ads they wanted (over three thousand were available), when they wanted. In the twenty-four hours following the 2000 Super Bowl, 1.8 million users downloaded more than twelve terabytes of streaming video—the equivalent, as Andrew Zipern noted in the *New York Times,* of over half the information in the Library of Congress.

What people like about advertising, in print or on TV, is simple. We like its ability to entertain while it informs us about new (or the same old) products. Advertisers like to reflect the desires of their audiences, and audiences, for their part, like to see their desires reflected. What we don't like about advertising is equally powerful. Advertising is unavoidable, intrusive, and pervasive in its relentless capacity to frame everything in life as a potential sale.

It is an old saw in city planning that population follows transportation. In advertising, ads follow media. Advertising multiplies in a direct ratio to the growth of information technologies, and that growth has been astounding.

In the '50s we had the technology to distribute a handful of general interest magazines, such as *Life, Look,* and *Saturday Evening Post.* By the '90s, we were publishing forty thousand titles and using specialized mailing lists to identify and justify the appropriate audiences. In the '60s, we were entertained and informed by three TV networks. By the end of the century we could choose from over five hundred channels.

In the 1980s, personal computers stood alone and functioned as fancy typewriters. Today the networked PC is giving way to the laptop, the laptop to the wireless networked personal digital assistant.

Each addition to the available media has turned the stream of advertising into a deluge and the deluge into a tsunami. Advertisers surround us with every kind of message in every possible way, to our increasing annoyance. Golfers don't just golf, and basketball players don't just shoot hoops. They compete while sporting the equivalent of sandwich boards (albeit subtly and tastefully designed) for their sponsors; team Nike v. team Adidas v. team Reebok. Meanwhile ordinary citizens gain status by wearing the signs and symbols of various haberdashers. Advertising tells us what a particular sign means. We wear the sign and let people know we are members of the community, followers of Calvin or Ralph or Giorgio or Gianni.

Great public gathering places used to be named for civic-minded public men (Shea Stadium in New York is one of the last remaining examples) or for the cities that supported them. Today they serve the advertising needs of companies that see them as very, very, very large billboards. From Staples Arena to 3Com Park to Bank One Ballpark, the culture of selling has become all-consuming.

You would think that people would have good feelings about something so essential to the success of the economy and the realization of their happiness. To a large extent they do. To a large extent they don't. Even an authority as neutral as *Webster's Dictionary* suggests why the ambivalence is deep.

The lexicographical gatekeepers who tell us what things mean can hardly find a nice thing to say about the verb *sell.* Whether by the base definition or the chosen example, whether unconsciously or consciously, they make it clear that selling is anything but an innocent behavior.

Selling, as Webster's sees it, is not something you tolerate because it helps you get the goods that make you happy. Selling is one small step from being—and this is no exaggeration—evil.

S E L L   **1:** to deliver or *give up in violation of duty, trust, or loyalty:* BETRAY—often used with *out* **2a:** (1): to give up (property) to another for money or other valuable consideration (2): to offer for sale **b:** to give up in return for something else esp. *foolishly or dishonorably (sold his birthright for a mess of pottage)* c: to exact a price for *(sold their lives dearly)* **3a:** *to deliver into slavery for money* **b:** to give into the power of another *(sold his soul to the devil)* **c:** to deliver the personal service of for money **4:** to dispose of or manage for profit *instead of in accordance with conscience, justice, or duty (sold his vote)* **5a:** to develop a belief in the trust, value, or desirability of : gain acceptance for (a campaign manager trying to sell his candidate **6:** to impose on: CHEAT (realized that he had been sold) . . .

Pursuing happiness has an almost idyllic, playful ring to it. But being sold the ideas that make you happy, being persuaded to purchase the objects that make you secure in your identity, is not a neutral transaction. It is dealing with the devil. This underlying sense that selling is evil is at the heart of the tension between the culture of high art and its darker siblings, otherwise known by labels like: low art, middlebrow culture, popular art, advertising, commercial illustration, and kitsch.

For a long time the barrier between the two cultures was crossed only at great peril to the reputation of the artist. That is not the case anymore. Beginning with the outrages of Dada in the first half of the twentieth century and continuing with the advent of pop art in the second half, great reputations have been forged by artists who made a point of ignoring the dividing line and working both sides at once. These were the painters and provocateurs who first saw the barrier not as a sacrosanct wall, but as a permeable membrane. They saw it as the artifact of a reactionary, conservative, hidebound art culture devoted to the values of the past and unwilling to confront the disturbing new values of the present.

Pop art, for instance, made advertising its subject. Pop's critics saw that as the essential problem. "Pop's social effect," Hilton Kramer said, "is simply to reconcile us to a world of commodities, banalities, and vulgarities—which is to say, an effect indistinguishable from advertising art."

Pop art did take its spirit from the bold, bald clarity of the advertising aesthetic. It sang the praises of commercial art with tunes of irony and respect. The pop aesthetic, rooted in the Dada of Duchamp and presaged in the early work of Stuart Davis, rejected the obscurity of abstract expressionism in favor of looking at things as they are, no matter how low or common or vulgar. It came bounding out of the jack-in-the-box of American culture in the works of Johns, Lichtenstein,

Oldenburg, and of course the man who plumbed the depths of the shallow with more abandon than any other, Warhol.

As has often been noted, virtually all of the painters who entered the pantheon of pop started out working the more narrow veins of advertising. They began as shoe designers, window decorators, illustrators, billboard painters, cartoonists. They went on, in one way or another, to turn the contents of their first jobs into the subject of their art. They painted what was in front of them every day. They painted what we were all seeing—soup cans, ads, beer cans, celebrities, and flags. They had the vibrancy and verve of a movement; the energy of popularity and success gave them a sense of exuberance that had little to do with the myth of the painter as someone who suffers for his art.

Nothing captures the vitality of this "new" art better than Claes Oldenburg's famous manifesto, now forty years old.

I am for an art. . .that does something other than sit on its ass in the museum. . .I am for an art that grows up not knowing it is art at all, an art given the chance of having a starting point of zero. I am for an art that embroils itself with everyday crap and still comes out on top. . .I am for U.S. Government Inspected art, Grade A art, Regular Price art, Yellow Ripe art, Extra-Fancy art, Ready-to-Eat art, Best-for-less art, Ready-to-cook art, Fully cleaned art, Spend Less art, Eat Better art, Ham art, pork art, chicken art, tomato art, banana art, apple art, turkey art, cake art, cookie art.

As with Oldenburg's sculptures, the sheer rhetorical inflation of the idea makes you smile. His use of purely commercial language to mark out the territory of art is at the heart of what this book is about.

Looking closely at the intertwining of art and selling allows us to see American culture in flux. We are caught in riptides of change that are as appealing as they are disorienting. After all, the perennial impulse of America is to encourage change by idolizing the new over the not-so-new and by

Outstanding advertising can be prepared best
when everyone concerned with it
has a fanatical belief
that a sales curve bending upward
is one of the world's most beautiful pictures.

YOUNG & RUBICAM, Inc., *Advertising*

New York · Chicago · Detroit · San Francisco · Hollywood · Montreal · Toronto · London

ignoring the old. Ironically enough, the passion for the new is itself nothing new. America's first and still sagest demographer, Alexis de Tocqueville, described the burgeoning American population of 170 years ago as the most freedom-loving, the most materialist, and the most religious he had ever encountered. These three qualities alone explain the persistent growth of advertising in American culture. They explain why people who make ads, who get paid to get the attention of these pious, freedom-loving materialists, find

Above: The tension between art and advertising shows clearly in this 1945 ad run by Young & Rubicam in *Fortune Magazine.* The hard-sell forces of business wanted to put art in its proper place.

images of high culture, icons of historical significance, portraits from the classical past, paintings of religious subjects—in fact, paintings of every class and type—reasonably practical tools for selling.

It is true that art (which hopes to be timeless) and advertising (which aims to be up-to-the-minute) have different goals, but they do share a certain impatience with the world. In advertising the span of time that gets the most attention is the short attention span. Artists, not seeing much future in doing what has been done before, are also looking for the next new thing. This shared eagerness and impatience have generated uncounted ads on the one hand and innumerable art movements on the other. The number of art movements that have careered through the last century is daunting, and each one has in some way interacted with the prolific advertising of our era. This is the context in which many artists have to think about their own work. Behind every school or movement or technique there have been artists who have had to consider how their art fit into a world whose values were best expressed in terms of markets, commodities, consumers, and sellers.

Some, of course, have ignored the world of advertising, some have railed against it, some have appropriated and co-opted it, and some have been co-opted by it. Even a selective list of these movements can leave you reeling.

Abstract expressionism. Action painting. Art brut. Ashcan school. Assemblage. Body art. Color-field painting. Computer art. Conceptual art. Dada. Cubism. Earth art. Fauvism. Feminist art. Fluxus. Found object. Happenings. Installation art. Kinetic sculpture. Kitsch. Minimalism. Modernism. Naïve art. Neo-Dada. Neo-expressionism. New wave. New York school. Op art. Performance art. Photo-realism. Pop art. Postmodernism. Primitivism. Realism. School of Paris. Social realism. Surrealism. Young British artists.

This book is less about the chronological history of the collisions between art and advertising and more about curiosity, impulse, and juxtaposition; less about words and more about images. It gives you a set of snapshots in time, hotlinks in perception, a gathering of subject matters and attitudes that are lenses that refresh something you have been looking at so long (the art), that you hardly even see it anymore. Conversely, these juxtapositions can give you a way to see something you see all the time but hardly ever notice (the advertising) in ways that might lead you to take a second look, a look that might enlarge your sense of the images and connections and consistencies and manipulations that is the cultural ecology we live in every day. The structure is intended not to march you down the alley of an argument, but to allow you to wander in the fields of your own curiosity.

I've tried to think in terms of a Web aesthetic. There are quotations from artists, critics, and advertising executives scattered throughout. Similarly, there are Web sites for artists, agencies, and clients. If something tickles your interest, get online and learn more.

The book asks two open-ended and inclusive questions: How have advertisers used "fine art" to sell their products? How has advertising influenced "fine art"? Each chapter begins with a spread that gives you a preview of what follows. Think of it as a home page or a site map to direct you to what interests you first. Taken together, the images that follow offer a kaleidoscopic view of the enveloping power of American mercantile culture over the last century. Sincere or ironic, witty or banal, motivating or manipulating, hard-sell or soft, highbrow or low, these are the signposts that direct us in our pursuit of happiness.

Opposite: Absolut's campaign in the 1980s and 1990s didn't just use art, it used all forms of art, made art the core meaning of its brand, and made clear that the border between fine art and advertising was a permeable membrane.

ABSOLUT MUSEUM.

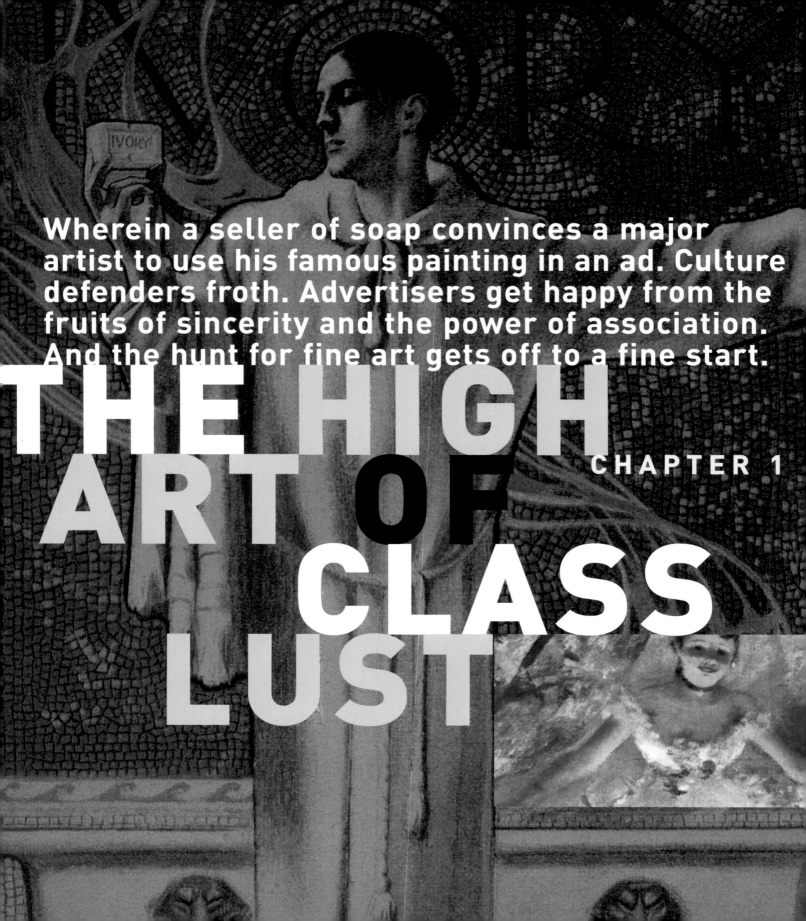

Wherein a seller of soap convinces a major artist to use his famous painting in an ad. Culture defenders froth. Advertisers get happy from the fruits of sincerity and the power of association. And the hunt for fine art gets off to a fine start.

THE HIGH ART OF CLASS LUST

"Advertising is the genie which is transforming America into a place of comfort, luxury, and ease for millions."
WILLIAM ALLEN WHITE

"Few people at the beginning of the nineteenth century needed an adman to tell them what they wanted."
JOHN KENNETH GALBRAITH

ARISTOCRATS, ACTRESSES, AND ANIMAL FAT.
Preachers, professors, and physicians.
PROMOTIONS, PAINTINGS, AND PUBLICITY STUNTS.

Aristocrats, actresses, and animal fat.

Preachers, professors, and physicians.

Promotions, paintings, and publicity stunts.

This is what ran through Thomas J. Barratt's head when he thought about selling Pears' soap to the newly minted middle class in Victoria's England. He should have been an American, because he understood better than most the motivating power of class lust. The tension between people of different classes is often characterized in economic terms as a conflict, or in cultural terms as a war. But in America, people spend less time pitting one class against another than they spend enticing, convincing, assuring, encouraging, and selling people on the fundamental belief that they, or at least their children, have a good chance of leaving their class and getting to a higher one.

America has been the social petri dish where the power of class lust and the energy of individualism have combined to create a profoundly commercial, status-driven social order populated by consumers and led by marketers and advertisers. And Thomas J. Barratt, although an Englishman, understood this dynamic in his bones, a reminder that America is, after all, the realized dream of Europeans who fled a class-bound world for one whose possibilities appeared boundless.

Barratt married into a soap-making family and became the son-in-law every father dreams of. He had so many seminal marketing ideas that he has actually been called the father of modern advertising. Although, unless you travel in academic circles, it's probably more accurate to call him the forgotten father of modern advertising.

Pears' soap was a transparent bar. Barratt aimed to associate it with cleanliness, purity, and high quality. He understood, before anyone, the need for consistency and persistence in advertising. And he was always open to trying whatever methods and means he could think of to sell his soap.

There was, for instance, no law against defacing foreign currency in England. Barratt had the idea of giving the public a way to buy his product with money that was branded with the name of his soap. He imported 250,000 French centimes, imprinted the name Pears' on them, and put them into circulation so customers could have the fun of paying for their bar of Pears' with money imprinted with the brand name. The ploy was a fair measure of how opportunistic Barratt was and how immature the international monetary system was. Parliament soon passed a law forbidding the practice.

Barratt invented the first full-blown national media testimonial campaign. He enlisted Sir Erasmus Wilson, president of the Royal College of Surgeons, to vouch that Pears' had none of the "objectionable properties of ordinary soap." Lillie Langtry, an actress who combined the esteem accorded Meryl Streep with the notoriety of Madonna, happily appeared without pay in print ads recommending Pears'. No one seemed to think that Miss Langtry's greatest role, as the mistress of the Prince of Wales, detracted from the Pears' brand image of purity and cleanliness. If that soap touched Lillie's skin, and Lillie was touched by the prince, then you could rise, for a moment, to royalty by association with the talisman that Pears' put in your hands.

In addition to branding money and using testimonial advertising, Barratt was virtually the first to understand the power of free samples and lifestyle demographics. For instance, whenever there was a birth announcement in the newspaper, he would have his marketing people send the young mother a free bar of Pears' and some literature to go with it.

But of all the things he did, the one that caused the most controversy and has had the most lasting notoriety was his use of a piece of fine art to sell his soap. Any survey of fine art and advertising has to begin here, with Barratt's idea to advertise his soap by using Sir John Everett Millais's *A Child's*

Opposite: *A Child's World* by Sir John Everett Millais was the first museum-quality painting to be used in advertising.

"Many a small thing has been made large by the right kind of advertising."

MARK TWAIN

World. Employing the painting in an ad caused much consternation among the guardians of high culture and initiated the arguments that we will see manifest again and again.

Millais didn't have much say in the transaction. A cultural fixture as central to his day as, say, Warhol was to his, Millais was named a Baronet in 1885 and elected President of the Royal Academy in 1896. As the preeminent portrait painter of the children of the Victorian aristocracy he earned commissions that were enviable by any standards. For painting the child of one of his clients, he took home the equivalent of $110,000. He had, in fact, sold his copyright of *A Child's World* to the *Illustrated London News* without protecting himself against the possibility of Barratt's innovative marketing tactic.

The new chromolithographic technologies had made it possible to mass-produce excellent color prints in the magazines and newspapers of the day, and *A Child's World* was sold to run in a special Christmas edition. Millais had been persuaded that having millions of people see even an image of the original would offer untold numbers the elevating experience that only art can provide. It was Sir William Graham, the owner of the *London News,* who sold those rights to Pears'. Barratt saw the angelic qualities of the child's visage as a perfect way to sell his soap. He convinced Millais to let him put a small bar of Pears' soap in the picture. Millais was upset, but in the end he agreed.

For all of the wringing of hands that ensued, it should be noted that the ad itself became a raging success. It, like others to follow, was taken and framed and hung on the walls of cottages and rooms throughout the British Empire. The image was so popular, it created a market in bric-a-brac, and today you can even traffic on eBay in cups and saucers and bowls imprinted with the Pears' *Bubbles* painting, as it was popularly renamed.

Likewise, it didn't hurt sales either. A closer look at the

Above and Opposite: Search **bubbles.org** for a history of Pears' soap. For an overview of the soap business, try **pharmj.com.**

For more on Millais, visit **victorianartinbritain.co.uk.** Also try **preraphaelites.co.uk.**

ad (see page 15) reveals one of the most popular and effective ways advertisers appropriate fine art for their selling message. Barratt's instincts were so clear that, despite the obvious datedness of the image, the principles he used became the guideline for all the best subsequent attempts to borrow the power of art to enhance the value of a considerably more vulgar product.

He keeps the product small and secondary. The bar of Pears' soap interpolated into the bottom right of the picture is close to actual size, even though that makes it less than obvious. The focus of the ad is still on the boy's face, transfixed by the bubble he has just sent off into the air. Yes, no doubt, a soap bubble, but we are left to figure that out for ourselves. The only help we get, judiciously placed, is the brand name itself as if the company were the painter signing the work.

Tasteful, clear, understated, the conjunction of art and commerce is not as jarring as it could have been. The painting, while altered, is not defaced, or made fun of. Your desire to associate with its value as an artifact from the reaches of the upper classes is left to work its magic, such as it may be.

Over time other practitioners will move away from this level of sincerity and sentimentality. But here, in this initial moment, the conjunction of the two worlds is actually touching. That little boy, like the man who painted him, has no idea what he has started.

Barratt, of course, did. And he took it further. He inserted his tag line into all sorts of painted worlds. He added copy to the *Bubbles* ad. And when he went on to commission other work, it often evoked the standards of classical oils. One peculiar scenario is notable if only because it is so much more bizarre than *Bubbles*.

It is an amalgamation of images from other paintings and other Pears' ads (see page 16). Here we aren't looking at a small, barely noticeable bar of Pears' soap. The soap in this ad

actually has angels' wings, to remind us that Pears' draws its own authority from an even higher power. If cleanliness is next to godliness, then Pears' isn't just a soap, it's a sacrament.

Where the *Bubbles* ad had the Pears' name as a signature, more like a part of the painting than the imprimatur of an advertiser, this painting gives Pears' full typographical expression. How you see the name on the box should be how you see it in the ad. The tag line "Good morning, have you used Pears' soap?" is embedded in the painting.

Before "Just do it," "A diamond is forever," "Good to the last drop," "Have it your way," "Reach out and touch someone," and "99 and $^{44}/_{100}$ percent pure," Barratt had made "Good morning, have you used Pears' soap?" the first brand slogan to be completely absorbed by an entire culture.

The painting draws us to a rich tableau that assumes an audience with the time and interest to get involved in its story. The young woman in the upper left-hand corner opens the window to her stately stone home and greets the day. In the foreground one tonsured monk promotes Pears' to a skeptical colleague who has, indeed, not used his Pears' today. Next to them a burdened nurse calms a baby while a naked two-year-old girl stands by, a little ashamed. In the background a hunched, possibly blind boy carries an oil painting of another delicate-skinned aristocratic woman; he is followed by one dark and one fair child. In the right foreground, closest to the reader, is the young boy from the *Bubbles* painting, still enamored with his bubbles, which are commingling with the angelic Pears' bars.

THE HONEYMOON
SIR EDWIN LANDSEER

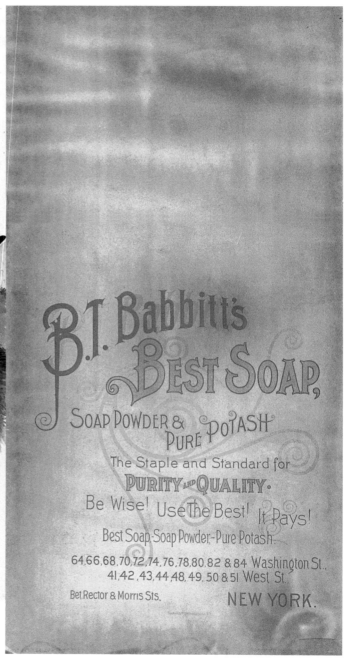

B.T. Babbitt's
BEST SOAP,
SOAP POWDER & PURE POTASH
The Staple and Standard for
PURITY AND QUALITY.
Be Wise! Use The Best! It Pays!
Best Soap-Soap Powder-Pure Potash.
64,66,68,70,72,74,76,78,80,82 & 84 Washington St.,
41,42,43,44,48,49,50 & 51 West St.
Bet.Rector & Morris Sts.   NEW YORK.

Above: Babbitt's, a Pears'
competitor, adapted the popular
animal paintings of Sir Edwin
Landseer as prints suitable for
framing. The sell was on the
back. Check **speel.demon.co.uk**
and **ephemerasociety.org**.
Opposite: J.C. Leyendecker's
illustration of an elegant bather
contemplating his bar of Ivory
soap never hung in a museum.
But its allusion to classical
Rome points out how much the
imagery of high art continued to
influence soap advertising.

· I V O R Y   S O A P ·
· I T   F L O A T S ·

Story paintings that incorporate the product are a staple for advertisers appropriating fine art. Barratt's strategy gave birth to a long line of ads featuring high-culture art altered to focus us on not-so-high-culture products. Some merely juxtapose the product with the painting, hoping the upper-class sheen of art will rub off on the product. Some insert the product in the painting; some use the painting to express an attitude appreciative of the product; some make fun of the painting through parody and satire; some show you how witty they are by how they use the painting.

All these strategies exist side by side. While irony and parody and satire come into their own after Marcel Duchamp and the Dada gang hoist the art world by its various petards, they never fully displace attempts to sincerely associate a product with the status of high art. In fact, from Barratt's first expropriation, the essential outcome of using museum art was not to spread the benefits of art to the masses—as Barratt convinced Millais he would—but to give the masses an avenue by which they could aspire to a higher class. Class lust is what motivates the appropriation of a work of high art to sell the work of mass production.

The roots of envy grow especially deep in the fertile loam of America's democratic materialism. From Vance Packard's *The Status Seekers* to David Brooks's ingenious piece of current-day anthropology, *Bobos in Paradise,* there is no shortage of observers to chronicle all the ways producers and purveyors (and the advertising agencies they hire) encourage people to yearn for a better place than the one they were born into.

Americans like to think of themselves as members of a classless society. When we consider other, more obviously class-bound societies, the idea has some merit. Any number of studies argue for the vitality of American class mobility. Many others purport to show how that mobility is more myth than fact. Either way, this inherent desire to find a place in the vast, flat social panorama of a society devoted to individualism has given advertisers more grist to mill than all the amber waves of grain America has ever harvested.

Today many advertisers are still happy to use art simply to illustrate to their customers that they are smart and upper class. Look, for instance, at a campaign that ran for a little-known software systems manufacturer, Sungard. Here art is used for its meaning not its popularity. Mercury and Hercules, as depicted in the little-known work of Coypel and Zurbaran, illustrate simple points about products and systems too complicated to describe. The lure is an association with intelligence, knowingness, and connoisseurship in business. A painting offers a sense of seriousness. The classical subject matter suggests wisdom and timelessness. The qualities of the gods evoked

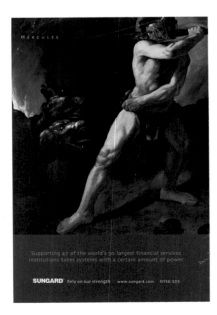

Above: Sungard® sells financial software. High art gives abstractions a noticeable emotional context and differentiates them from competitors who run pictures of people in offices.

are the content that we are to associate with the advertiser. Mercury
signifies that the company's success
reflects a "strong sense of mission,"
and from Hercules we are to con-
clude that selling "systems" to the
world's largest financial institutions
takes "a certain amount of power."

The evocation of such abstractions is the art director's way of taking
the simple claim provided by the
client and giving it visual drama. The
fact that the art here has nothing to
do with banking, with software, or the systems that "e-process"
stuff suggests how difficult it was to find something to say
about this company that would clarify what it does.

A more successful use of art that is not that well known
but at least works to express the essence of the brand can be
seen in an ad that introduced Tabu in 1931. The sense of
romance here is not sexy in the adolescent, androgynous way
of today's Opium or Eternity. But the ad continues to feel available to a contemporary sensibility. It illustrates one of the
selling arguments for using "timeless" art: your product is not
only associated with high culture, it becomes part of an eternal
world where values are true and unchanging and things are
not as ephemeral as cosmetics and cosmetic advertising
actually are.

A painting by the not particularly famous French painter
René Prinet titled *The Kreutzer Sonata* evoked a moment of
overwhelming passion no doubt motivated by Tabu, the forbidden
fragrance. The concept still works. Since 1931 Tabu has played
variations on that theme, adapting to shifts in cultural norms
and expectations. In a recent version the accompanist is now a
female artist and the soloist is her model, a naked Adonis who
has gotten off his chair to bend her backward in an embrace

worthy of the cover of a romance novel.

These ads not only use art, they are about the nature of
the artist. Artists are more in touch with their emotions; they
are more expressive; they are free of the restraints of social
propriety; they even work with the naked. This idea of the
artist as the embodiment of emotional freedom underlies a
lot of the consumer ads, especially in the cosmetic world, that
use paintings or evoke the qualities of the artistic
personality.

From systems software to perfume, many advertisers
have been content to follow in Baratt's footsteps. But that was not
the only tactic. Over time, other advertisers decided that the best
way to use art was to have fun with it. Their thinking was simple.
They would get noticed because they were irreverent.

And you would like them, and their
products, because you shared a willingness
to have fun with art. In short, when it
came to using high art in advertising,
a little irony would go a long way.

Above: Tabu used art to point to
the timelessness of art and love:
"If you want to inspire something
lasting, do it with something that
lasts." To see what goes into

selling perfume, visit **jolique.com.**
Tabu was relaunched in 2000.
See **jabaslublu.com/Dana** for
an update.

Campari. Reflection on art.

Here, you will find not only one of the most inviting places to stay, but also the most unique insight on where you might wish to go. Only at The St. Regis.

THE ST. REGIS
New York

Opposite: *The Bar at the Folies-Bergére* by Edouard Manet portrayed a taciturn bargirl/prostitute. Did Campari expect its target audience to know that

she was expected to do more than serve drinks?
Above: Degas's impressionist canvas of dancers viewed from the orchestra gives the St. Regis

Hotel an artful way to say they can find you entertainment as elegant as your room.

Above: High art may be timeless, but it can still be brought up-to-date. United Airlines took George Seurat's *La Grande Jatte* and respectfully added a few thousand dots to the picture to say; then or now, Paris deserves a visit.

The David is clothed and great paintings are altered greatly. Meanwhile the aspiration of art is embraced by the inspiration of humor. Parody plays while satire bites its own tail. Or, how the sincerity of platitudes is crowded out by the irony of attitudes.

THE IRONIC

CHAPTER 2

GET
GOING

Lemon.

"The art of the past no longer exists as it once did. Its authority is lost."

J O H N   B E R G E R

"I honestly believe that advertising is the most fun you can have with your clothes on."

J E R R Y   D E L L A   F E M I N A

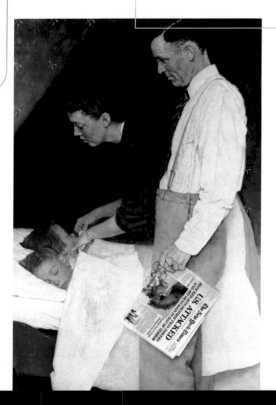

"Living in an age of advertisement, we are perpetually disillusioned."

J. B.   P R I E S T L Y

HE'S SEXY

And until you've seen him in person, it's hard to appreciate just how attractive he really is.

He's tall. He's sexy. And until you've seen him in person, it's hard to appreciate just how attractive he really is.

Ask anyone who's walked down the corridor at the Accademia in Florence, past the rough-hewn sculptures Michelangelo never finished, and entered the Rotunda and gazed upon the *David*, standing some seventeen feet tall.

With one long, languorous, anatomically incorrect arm resting by his side and the other raised to his head, with his well-articulated sex organ enjoying its proper place, with his perfectly chiseled deltoids and gorgeously wry smile bathed in the natural light, the *David* has defined a space of youthful, athletic male sensuality that has no peer. He is the model for all the male models whose job is to sell Calvin's underwear or Ralph's bathing suits.

The *David*, unlike other works of high art, is rarely borrowed by advertisers for its dignity and beauty. The role of the *David* is rather to give us something naked so we can make fun of the fact that male nakedness is forbidden. In advertising, the *David* is not an object to be venerated and respected. He is a friend to be joked with. He is most effective as a means to reach an audience that appreciates the art of irony, as Levi Strauss demonstrated years ago.

Levi's jeans started off as workmen's overalls, imbued with working-class grit and the sturdy manliness of the American West. They embodied the cowboy life, and as they traveled across the expanse of the twentieth century, they crossed more perceptual borders than any one pair of pants has a right to. Levi's have transcended their origin as mere clothing and become icons in their own right.

Denim was the cloth of working people, and jeans became the first democratic clothing to move from the lower class to the middle class and ultimately to live in the idealized world of classless America. After Levi's jeans came

Above: Go to **levistrauss.com /about/history/denim** for a quick history of denim, jeans, and the growth of the Levi's brand.

khaki pants and the ultimate icon of the meritocracy, the Gap T-shirt.

Utilitarian and functional, Levi's jeans migrated into a world of male sexiness and cowboy roughness. Riding the burgeoning consumer culture of the 1960s, fueled by the baby-boomer version of teenage revolt, they became the uniform for dressing down when adult culture demanded dressing up. Levi's were the clothing of the counterculture's *sans culottes*, but that was only a way station in their evolution. They moved on to become the form-fitting, sexy pants of suburban rebels. By the 1970s the female market for jeans was approaching the size of the male market. Once marketers had flooded the stores with multiple brands and various fits, from stone-washed to flared to hip-hugger and back again, Levi's faced the problem of maintaining their dominant share. Because advertising's role is to express differences where they exist (which is rare) and to make you perceive differences where they don't, it strains to be outrageous when the market is saturated, distribution is wide, and margins are shrinking.

Softer, Thicker, Unusually Durable And Almost Unshrinkable.

Bassett-Walker Sturdy Sweats Can Make Anybody Look Like A Jock.

And that is often when irony enters the picture. If you can't differentiate your product, then make fun of it or at least have fun while you're asking people to buy it.

Living as we do in an age where irony is pervasive, it is easy to forget that irony was not always a ready-made tool for advertisers. In fact, the Age of Irony in advertising begins with Doyle, Dane, and Bernbach's famous campaign for Volkswagen. The two most famous ads, "Think Small" and "Lemon," were the opposite of everything car advertisements had been about up to that moment. And while more conventional, straightforward advertising hasn't disappeared, irony has taken over, especially when advertisers want to reach younger consumers.

So it's hardly a surprise to see the *David*, the epitome of naked sensuality, used to make fun of adult prudishness, in particular regarding sexuality, as a way of appealing to a younger audience's more liberal attitudes. This *David* isn't even wearing new jeans, or ironed jeans, or stylized jeans. They are old cutoff jeans. They are mutilated and worn and ready-to-be-thrown-out jeans. But they do have one last function. They are the denim fig leaf that turns the *David* from a distant piece of stone into a rather attractive contemporary.

Above: Grant Woods's *American Gothic* ranks with the *Mona Lisa* as a work of art advertisers find endless ways to have fun with.

Make sense of our times.

The New York Times
Expect the World®
nytimes.com

Make sense of our times.

The New York Times
Expect the World®
nytimes.com

This Spread: The irony of altering Norman Rockwell's evocations of an idealized American past to make sense of the world after the attack on the World Trade Center has earned this campaign numerous awards. Rockwell, famous as an illustrator, now enjoys exhibitions at museums such as the Guggenheim. This is an example of advertising art making the journey to the venues of high art. Go to **bozell.com** for more.

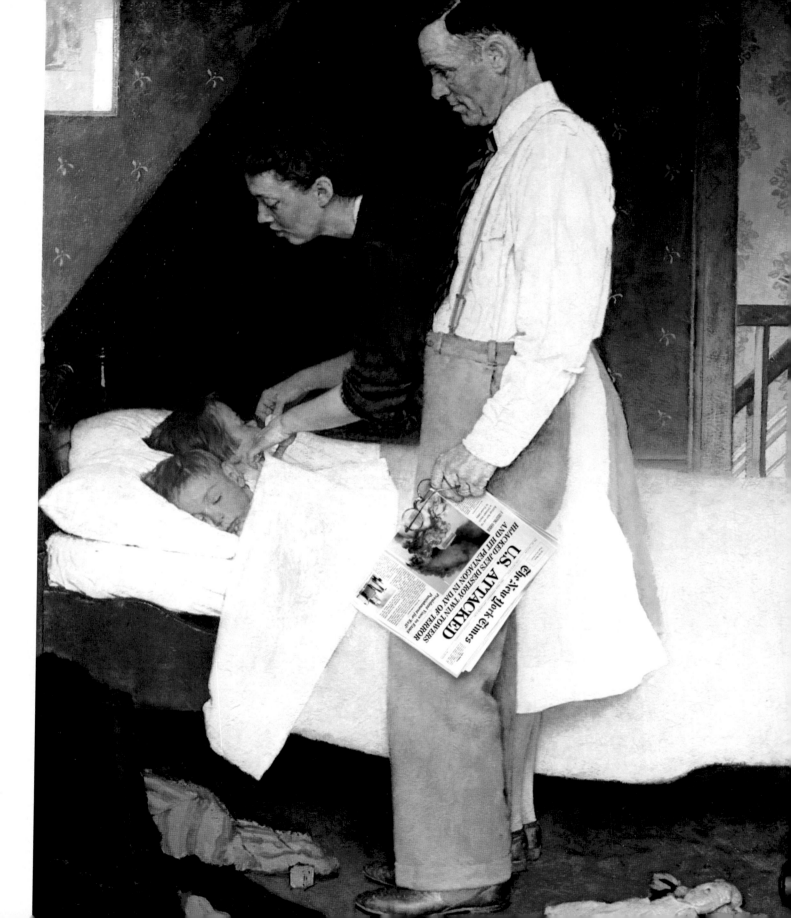

Lemon.

This Volkswagen missed the boat.
The chrome strip on the glove compartment
is blemished and must be replaced. Chances
are you wouldn't have noticed it; Inspector
Kurt Kroner did.
There are 3,389 men at our Wolfsburg factory with only one job: to inspect Volkswagens
at each stage of production. (3000 Volkswagens
are produced daily; there are more inspectors

than cars.)
Every shock absorber is tested (spot check-
ing won't do), every windshield is scanned.
VWs have been rejected for surface scratches
barely visible to the eye.
Final inspection is really something! VW
inspectors run each car off the line onto the
Funkstandprüfstand (car test stand), tote up 189
check points, gun ahead to the automatic

brake stand, and say "no" to one VW out of
fifty.
This preoccupation with detail means the
VW lasts longer and requires less maintenance, by and large, than other cars. (It also
means a used VW depreciates
less than any other car.)
We pluck the lemons; you get
the plums.

Although it may be an unintended outcome, the ads in
this chapter are never driven by satire—a genre that pokes
holes in its subject by making it look ridiculous. The different
ways advertisers use high art may make it look ridiculous, but
that is only if you don't get the joke. Similarly, there is very
little that can be properly labeled as parody. Advertisers imi-
tate serious works, and in many instances they have fun doing
so, but their intent is rarely to point out some incongruous
meaning in the original.

The irony you see in the examples here is derived directly
from the irony DNA of the Volkswagen ads of the early '60s.
"Lemon," more than any other ad, and that campaign more
than any other campaign, offers a simple tutorial in the commercial uses of irony as advertising sees it. At its heart irony
works by saying the opposite of what it means. It is the opposite

of sincerity, and therefore became the next selling strategy
for advertisers who recognized that sincerity was losing its
ability to persuade a population inundated by advertisements.
Everyone knew that, by definition, *selling* means shaving the
truth, promising more than you can deliver, hoping for the
best, ignoring the complex. Simply and directly expressing
your product's unique selling proposition started to lose its
force of argument. While this selling philosophy never disappeared, the campaign thinking it fathered, like "Ring Around
the Collar" or "Please Don't Squeeze the Charmin," became
less and less likely to work.

Selling with a wink, entertaining the audience while
conveying the message indirectly, being wry rather than
straightforward became a counter strategy. It was an easy
strategy to execute during the rise of the counterculture. This
vast generation forged its identity in opposition to all authority
and marched under the banner, "Don't trust anyone over
thirty." The baby-boom demographic gave advertisers an
encouraging context for moving away from the conservative,
tried-and-true, hard sell to the liberal, easier-to-misunder-
stand, and harder-to-measure soft sell.

Very little of what you see here could have run before the
1960s. Many of the paintings of religious scenes seem oblivi-
ous of the offense they may give to anyone who thinks that the
need to sell a product doesn't justify desecrating sacred
images and icons. Others follow the simple Pears' soap technique of slipping the product into the picture. The interplay
between the painters' sensibility and the advertisers vary.

But what is constant is the way the power of irony and the appeal of high art combine
to persuade, provoke, and evoke in order to sell everything from birth control to
booze, from newspapers to running shoes.

Above: Irony in advertising
begins with Doyle, Dane, and
Bernbach's Volkswagen campaign. They trusted the audience
to understand that the ad meant

the opposite of what it said.
Opposite: James McNeill
Whistler's painting of his mother
is often tapped by advertisers.
Mercedes-Benz takes its turn,

using a three-page ad to ask you
to buy their car because it will
make you even more "noticed"
than "one of the most recognizable
figures" in the world.

Once you drive one, there's no turning back.

Mercedes-Benz

Adds a little cheer to any mealtime. Tela Table paperwear

By comparison, any sin you've ever committed is garden variety.

The Episcopal Church

Above (top): Sacred religious subject matter is fair game for many advertisers. Da Vinci's *The Last Supper* offers a perfect setting for any company that wants to draw attention to mundane mealtime products. The hero of this campaign couldn't be less heroic: the paper napkin.

Above (bottom): This 1980s campaign by Fallon/McElligott helped put that small Minneapolis agency on the map. Albrecht Dürer's depiction of the fall of mankind into sin lets the Episcopal Church expand its congregation by targeting its audience (sinners) and selling its most popular product (forgiveness).

Thanks, but I already know.

The most efficient pregnancy test.

Above: Fra Angelico's *Annunciation* depicts Gabriel giving Mary the news of her pregnancy. For those of us who experience intercourse with partners who are less than divine, this alternative pregnancy test will have to suffice.

Above: Nike's elaborate poster campaign for Inter-Milan, the soccer team they sponsor, emulates the style of Caravaggio. Each competitor's iconic mascot flees the serpent representing Nike's team. The drama of good and evil fits nicely with the mythology of sport. **Opposite:** Conflict, terror, and pain are emotions appropriate to Baroque painting and to sports. For Canal+, art also emphasizes their TV shows as ones that "turn basketball into an art form."

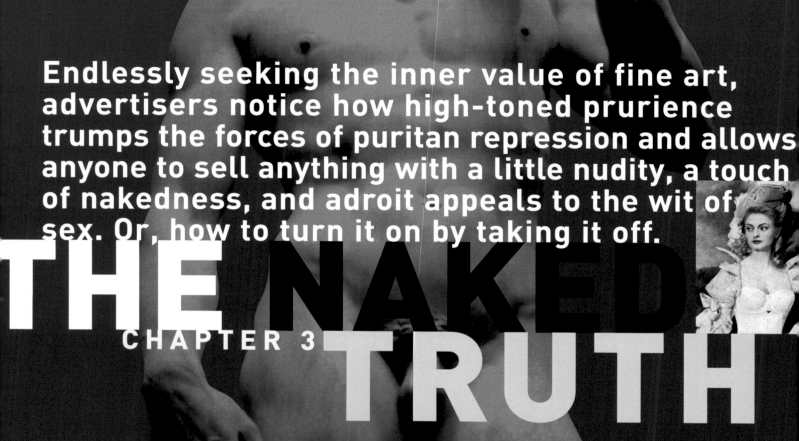

Endlessly seeking the inner value of fine art, advertisers notice how high-toned prurience trumps the forces of puritan repression and allows anyone to sell anything with a little nudity, a touch of nakedness, and adroit appeals to the wit of sex. Or, how to turn it on by taking it off.

THE NAKED TRUTH

CHAPTER 3

"Nakedness reveals itself. Nudity is placed on display . . . The nude is condemned to never being naked. Nudity is a form of dress."

JOHN BERGER

"Society drives people crazy with lust and calls it advertising."

JOHN LAHR

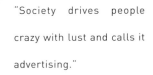

"Reader, beware of eccentricity when you advertise to people who are not eccentric."

DAVID OGILVY

It may be the most tired truism in advertising. **But that's only because it's one truth advertisers never find tiresome.**

Sex sells.

It may be the most tired truism in advertising, but only because it's one truth that advertisers never find tiresome. The use of fine art images has always allowed advertisers to invoke sexuality when there was no other way possible. Nude is permissible where naked is taboo.

Americans do sometimes confuse the two. In the first months after the attack on the World Trade Center, Attorney General John Ashcroft found himself giving numerous press conferences from the Justice Department briefing room. Directly behind him stood a statue of Justice with one breast exposed. Ashcroft ordered that the exposed breast of the statue be covered with a curtain.

Given the pervasiveness of sex as entertainment, and as a selling tool, Ashcroft's prudishness highlighted a tension in American life that advertisers are always aware of. Nude images from high art are a sort of visual euphemism; they allow advertisers to evoke sex without resorting to the vulgarity of nakedness. In a culture like America's, where puritanism and prurience are joined at the hip to libidinal desire and unrepentant repression, it stands to reason that advertisers would be happy to use a highbrow image to get away with a lowbrow tease. If anyone objects, there is ample cover under the mantel of upper-class appreciation. Objections offered by critics from the Ashcroft school can be readily dealt with: That's not a naked woman, that's a classical nude. That's not vulgar sex, that's timeless art. That's not meretricious advertising, that's beauty.

People laughed at Ashcroft because he mistook a nude statue from the world of fine art for a fine woman from the actual world. Seeing him as part hick, part philistine, part religious zealot, part tittering adolescent, and all prude, they laughed because he played to the stereotype of the sexually uptight, breast-obsessed, all-American man/boy.

"Art, like morality, consists in drawing the line somewhere."

G. K. CHESTERTON

For a long list of definitions and descriptions of what levels of nudity, nakedness, sex, and such are acceptable to one group that monitors American culture, try the movie guide available at **family-style.com.**

Most of the ads gathered here also use nudity to laugh at our general nervousness about inappropriate public nakedness. A look through this chapter reveals a whole set of contradictory attitudes towards sex and nakedness.

Some of these ads, for instance, simply evoke the beauty of the nude.

Some offer a nude body to inspire a nervous giggle.

Some use male nudity to poke fun at prudery.

Some use paintings of nude women to signal that this ad is directed only to women who want to learn about new developments in personal hygiene.

Some use nudity to conjure the power of the flirtatious female.

Some use nudity because their product has something to do with intercourse.

But in all these cases the advertiser could not photograph a naked man or a woman because that would be vulgar and pornographic. The painted image of a nude or the sculpted body carries the imprimatur of art and takes the prurience out. Art transforms forbidden bodies into perfectly acceptable selling arguments.

Of course the photo of naked men and women has been common in European advertising for a long time. It has certainly gained more currency in America in recent years in such places as fashion and cosmetic advertising. The pages of *Vogue* are ripe with nakedness and sexuality that make many of the ads here from earlier periods seem more quaint than provocative. But even today, if you want the benefit of a naked body then using a painted nude is still likely to generate fewer objections. HERE ARE SOME TO STUDIOUSLY OGLE.

Artbooks.com, bookstorming.com, printedmatter.org, artkrush.com, and **artincontext.com** are good sites for finding books and info about fine arts.

Following Spread: *Bunte* is the *People* magazine of Germany. As a tell-it-all celebrity magazine they use show-it-all art to entice new readers with an example of how they would treat Cleopatra's scandalous story.

Why it all ended with Caesar.
How she suffered.

She would have told all in BUNTE.

Cleopatra (69 – 30 BC)

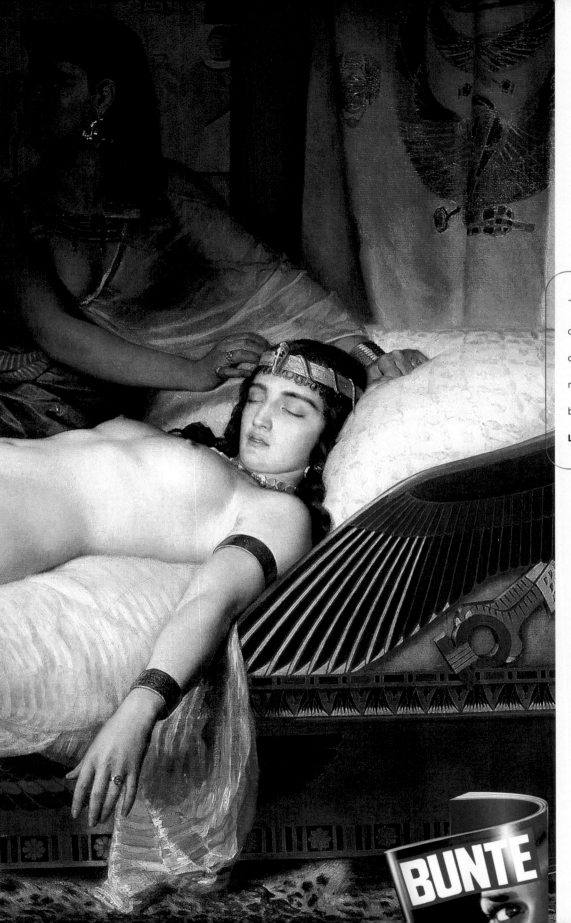

"I am one who believes that one of the greatest dangers of advertising is not that of misleading people, but that of boring them to death."
LEO BURNETT

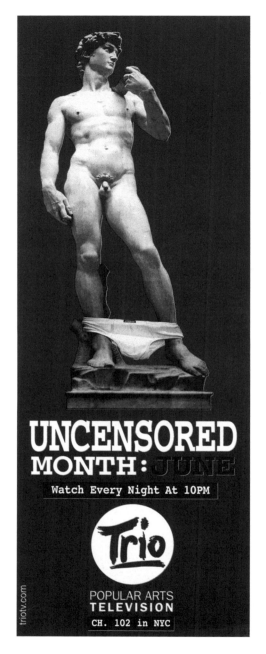

UNCENSORED
MONTH: JUNE

Watch Every Night At 10PM

Trio

POPULAR ARTS
TELEVISION
CH. 102 in NYC

triotv.com

For starters, there's always the *David.*
If you have a sexual product, he's your man. Indeed, the rise of the gay market has increased his popularity as a sales tool.

The *David* is the best known piece of fig-leaf-free statuary ever chiseled, and any advertiser who finds merit in full-frontal male nudity usually finds some way to exploit the shocking fact of that nakedness by invoking the timeless beauty of his nudity.

The sheer nakedness of the *David* can also be used to comment on and even provoke censorship. Here, Trio, a cable TV station, promotes its "Uncensored Month" by turning the ancient statue into a young man with his underwear down by his ankles. The ad ran this way in an alternative weekly, but it had a black bar covering the genitals when it appeared on the sides of busses.

In an earlier time, advertisers were clear that art was art and that nudity was not nakedness. One of the earliest examples of a nude statue in an ad had nothing to do with sex, instead the ad was about families. Positioning themselves as the best cereal for a family breakfast, this early ad for Kellogg's Corn Flakes uses the *Venus* to show how desirable the cereal is. The joke is that she can't satisfy her desire because she has no arms. The fact that she is naked from the waist up is incidental.

"In America sex is an obsession, in other parts of the world it is a fact."
**M A R L E N E
D I E T R I C H**

Above: The *David* is still the only way advertisers ever choose to show full frontal male nudity, whether in the United States or even in the considerably less restrictive world of European media.
Opposite: The *Venus de Milo*, saved from the kiln in 1820, stands in the Louvre as an epitome of classical beauty. The family image of Kellogg's brand Corn Flakes remains wholesome despite her nakedness.

If
Venus
Had
Arms

NONE GENUINE WITHOUT THIS SIGNATURE

W. K. Kellogg

classic
beauty

modern milk
multi-vitamin skin nutrition

There is, of course, more than one way to use a Venus, just as there was more than one way to portray her. Botticelli's *Birth of Venus*, like da Vinci's *Mona Lisa*, is one of the most readily referenced paintings in all of advertising. Her beauty travels well over the centuries, and the fantasy setting—she rises on a shell out of the sea—has made her attractive to all sorts of advertising suitors.

On the corporate side, she does business in the unlikely company of Shell Oil (see page 48). Her nudity

A SUBJECT YOU MAY NEVER
HAVE DISCUSSED WITH ANYONE.

Gyne-
Moistrin

here is made more acceptable by her own evident propriety, as she herself covers her bare necessities. This is, Shell tells us, one of a series of ads based on "seashell-inspired art treasures." The twists and turns of the copy are acrobatic, but in the end the reason for using this painting is simple. Venus is on a shell. Shell has a shell for a logo.

Using Venus but ignoring her nakedness allows all kinds of products to evoke the essence of femininity. Following in the time-honored strategy of identifying a problem in order to make money curing it, the makers of Gyne–Moistrin used fine art to speak about subjects that generally don't get spoken about in public.

The *Odalisque*'s back is turned towards us, the slightly furtive, slightly embarrassed look in her eye as she shifts her position lets us know that we are talking about something delicate, something female and personal and hidden: "A subject you may never have discussed with anyone."

Just as the upper-class imprimatur of fine art can be used to bring a sense of adult seriousness to subjects that are too personal to talk about, it can also be used to play with the titillating emotions of exposure. Nudity is made playful as well as provocative.

More recently, Ikea has given the Venus a fresh treatment. Utilitarian and iconoclastic in its concept, attitude, and imagery, Ikea is the no-nonsense, come-and-get-it, put-it-together-yourself furniture store from Sweden. Its products are known for good design and clean lines. Ikea's advertising has always been contemporary and provocative. They've garnered a great deal of awareness by running a TV commercial portraying two gay young men trying out beds for their new apartment. When they chose to use nudity in one of their ads, they naturally used it to express the essence of their brand.

Above and following pages: Botticelli's *Venus* uses her hands to modestly cover her nakedness while Zephyr gently blows her to shore. This combination of mod-esty and whimsy has made her popular among advertisers who use art to evoke female beauty. An ad from the 1940s invokes the nakedness of Venus and the phallic strength of classical columns to sell lingerie.

It's your world. **IKEA** Live better.

The Birth of Venus. Sandro Botticelli, 1478; Uffizi Gallery, Florence, Italy.

Foto arte e colore – Milano

The artist turns to nature to inspire his craftsmanship

Botticelli chose the mythical birth of Venus as a subject worthy of his brush and produced a masterpiece. Before then and since then most art has shown a preoccupation with the things of nature and the legends surrounding them. The seashell has for long held a fascination for the artist and served as his inspiration. But inspiration alone is not enough; it must be coupled with skilled craftsmanship to achieve perfection.

Scientists, as well as painters, know this problem, for it is their task to equate the inspiration and the offerings of nature with the things man can use.

At Shell, hundreds of scientists are engaged in the task of turning ideas inspired by nature's hidden petroleum stores into substances useful to man. This imaginative research results in products that perform better, last longer and cost less. Millions know these products by the sign of the familiar shell.

SHELL

The Shell Companies

Shell Oil Company
Shell Chemical Company
Shell Pipe Line Corporation
Shell Development Company
Shell Oil Company of Canada, Ltd.

This Ikea ad (see page 47) gives us the nude and naked together. High art, a suburban woman, and an almost rural setting are happily juxtaposed to make you think about the relationship between them and to evoke a feeling of independence and freedom. Venus is rising on her shell, all right, but this time she is an al fresco fresco on the side of a wall. Sitting in front of her is a modern, albeit more corpulent, Venus. She is flowing with flesh, Rubenesque, and happy, sunning herself on her own private nudist farm, enjoying tea in her deck chair (available, no doubt, at an Ikea outlet near you). Suggesting freedom from conventional behavior and conventional modern notions of beauty as well as a kinship with Botticelli's iconic evocation of classical beauty, the ad asks you to shop at Ikea not just for its furniture but for its sensibility.

Probably the most famous example of a campaign that uses the idea of nudity (rather than actual nudes) to create a bond with its target audience was the Maidenform ads of the 1950s. Maidenform's "I dreamed I was . . . in my Maidenform bra" was the sort of campaign that had, as they say in the business, legs. There was no end of situations in which a dreamlike fantasy of being undressed could be combined with talk about the benefits of the Maidenform bra.

In the two examples here, our heroines are transported into the world of fine art itself. "I dreamed I was a Work of Art in my Maidenform bra" puts the dreamer in a Gainsborough painting, where she can lord it over an English estate in her dishabille. The even more provocative "I dreamed I was Venus de Milo in my Maidenform bra" gives Venus back her arms only to put her in charge of a hip-high, one-armed young man whose partially good arm is used as a hanger for the blouse she has taken off. The bra will give your figure, the ad says, the "touch of Venus." Exactly what the touch is doing to the miniature young man is, however, not clear.

For the figure of the ages, Maidenform's new Pre-Lude* Once-Over lifts your curves, snugs in your waist...moulds you to the figure of your dreams. It's beautifully, comfortably strapless! Features the amazing contour band that swoops 'under-and-up' for a completely new kind of uplift! The quick-hook back-band makes for split second closing! Of course the garters are detachable! So, for your next really important 'dress up' occasion — give your figure a touch of Venus. Choose the fabric you want — but always choose Pre-Lude Once-Over.

White cotton broadcloth, 7.95; with new six-way straps, 8.95. White embroidered nylon, 10.95. Bridal white or cocktail black nylon lace, 12.50. A, B and C cups.

I dreamed I was Venus de Milo in my

maidenform bra

Opposite and Above: **Gainsborough.org** can show you more of the upper class English cachet being borrowed. For a

short history of Maidenform as a business, go to **americanhistory. si.edu/archives.**

[50 | 51]
Chapter 3 / THE NAKED TRUTH

Fine art nudes can be very effective in creating a sense of identity or in making a point by having some fun. All the Robin Bruce furniture brand needed in order to give their chairs an aura of intimacy and personality was a touch of Hopper and a reference to Ingres. Putting the chairs into the paintings beautifully renders the sense of thoughtfulness, of aloneness and privacy, without descent into bathos. The fact that much of the audience may not be able to name the painter or the painting doesn't matter. Renaming the chair for the new owner and telling you the price at which she bought it—Rachel's Chair $750—leverages the intimacy of the image directly on the point of the ad.

Of course, fine art nudity can also be used to show sex itself. Rest Assured mattresses use illustrations from the *Kama Sutra* to suggest that their mattress offers more pleasure than sex itself. The tag line, "Beds so comfortable you can't help falling asleep," is underscored by the fact that the women have their eyes closed.

Sex and nudity are used to point to the product benefit in a lighthearted way that uses humor to deflate whatever prurience the prudish might construe.

Employing fine art nudes has proved effective for advertisers of intimate products. It's also given advertisers of less likely products an opportunity to tickle the sensibilities of their audiences with images that offer the kind of provocative fun that even the likes of John Ashcroft might appreciate.

Above: Seeing people naked in their homes isn't prurient when the bodies we peer at are borrowed from works by Hopper and Ingres.

Opposite: Rest Assured mattress offers a clear example of images that would not be tolerated as photography but are acceptable because they are artifacts of high culture and ancient wisdom.

RESTASSURED

Beds so comfortable you can't help falling asleep.

RESTASSURED

Beds so comfortable you can't help falling asleep.

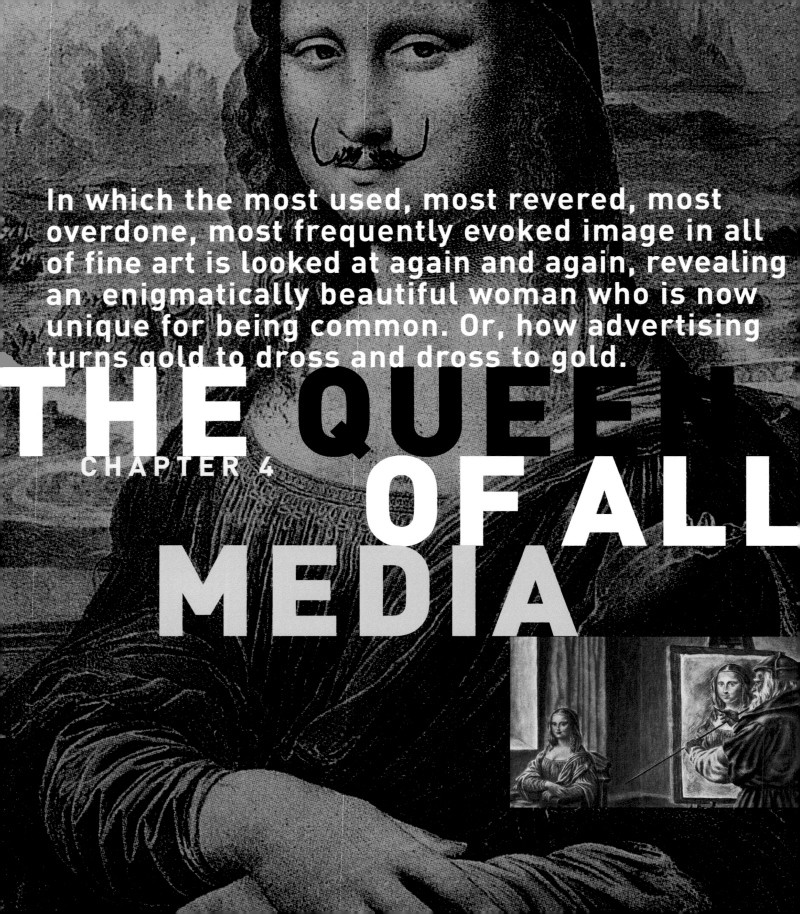

In which the most used, most revered, most overdone, most frequently evoked image in all of fine art is looked at again and again, revealing an enigmatically beautiful woman who is now unique for being common. Or, how advertising turns gold to dross and dross to gold.

THE QUEEN OF ALL MEDIA

CHAPTER 4

"To me it was merely a serene and subdued face, and there an end. There might be more in it, but I could not find it."

MARK TWAIN

"A fame as great as that of Leonardo's *Mona Lisa* is not an unmixed blessing for a work of art."

E. H. GOMBRICH

"The smile of the *Mona Lisa*, is it not again the same half ironic smile of the human soul that parades in peace as it looks upon a world liberated from human terror?"

EDGAR QUINET

No one has her reputation. No one has her scope or popularity. No painting and no woman has left the protective walls of the museum world and been embraced by more different elements of the new world of media than *La Giaconda,* a.k.a. the *Mona Lisa.*

The number of parodies and spoofs, restaurants and songs, magazine and matchbook covers, and posters has ranged beyond counting, although Donald Sassoon, in *Becoming Mona Lisa* has done his definitive best to track down as many of her appearances as seems humanly possible.

She wasn't always so popular. Before she became an emblem of how mechanical reproduction can create an audience whose size and interest beggars most artists' wildest hopes, the *Mona Lisa* was just another well-respected painting. True, she was already famous as a symbol of enigmatic beauty. Other artists had already used her as a model. However, her rise to the top didn't really begin until she was stolen from the walls of the Louvre in 1911.

Brought to the attention of the public at large through tabloid headlines and the general sense of outrage her theft inspired, the *Mona Lisa* achieved that most galvanizing characteristic, notoriety. She became a symbol of establishment art, and an object to make fun of.

When Marcel Duchamp drew a mustache and goatee on her face and titled his 'creation' *L.H.O.O.Q.*, it was an announcement to the commercializing world that this previously sacrosanct image was fair game for any sort of desecration. After all, she had already been stolen and defaced. How bad could it be to use her in an advertisement?

Where Michelangelo's *David* became an object of nervous, prudish, adolescent fun because he embodied the beauty of male nakedness, *Mona* became the number-one image to use when you wanted to make fun of establishment art. She is, of course, still often borrowed just for her cultural cachet. The lust for *Lisa*'s upper-class visage has remained remarkably constant over the last century. However, you are more likely to encounter her these days rendered in the spirit of Duchamp; *Mona* is the female image advertisers choose to have fun with when they want you to buy their product.

Indeed, when you start to catalog *Mona*'s popularity in the annals of advertising, you have to wonder if art directors and copywriters have the world's shallowest view of art history. Why do they choose *Mona* again and again whenever they need an image from high culture? It's as obvious as the nose on her face; her much discussed "enigmatic" smile.

Original. Chunky.

When we make Prince Spaghetti Sauce, we give you a choice. Because no two people have quite the same taste. P:

Above: Plumping up the *Mona Lisa* is only one way a little irreverence can turn high art to meet commercial needs. For a comprehensive window to all the uses of Mona in popular culture **studiolo.org** is indispensable.

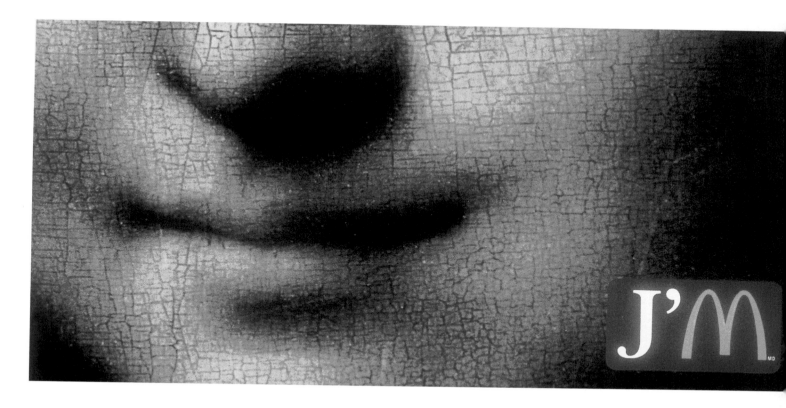

Look, for instance, at the McDonald's poster and the ad for Prince spaghetti sauce. Here the smile has not a jot of enigma about it. It is the smile of appetite. And in the case of Prince spaghetti sauce, *La Giaconda* is fast-forwarded into the image of an Italian mother whose love of pasta has clearly overwhelmed her love of her own svelte beauty; the shortest distance between *Mona* and Mama is a jar of Prince sauce.

The smile conveys satisfaction, AND ADVERTISERS LOVE NOTHING BETTER THAN AN ENDORSEMENT FROM A SATISFIED USER.

Because it is mysterious, *Mona Lisa*'s smile can be turned to any number of ends. Besides her appetite having been fulfilled, it can equally represent her appetite yearning

Above: Letting the enigmatic reputation of *Mona*'s smile speak for your product is among the most popular tactics.
Following Spread: When

Marcel Duchamp drew a mustache and goatee on the *Mona Lisa* he signed it with a provocative set of letters L. H. O. O. Q. which, when spoken in French,

say *Elle a chaud en cul* ("She's hot in the ass"). His deflation of this icon of high art made *Mona* free game for advertisers.

L H O O Q

to be fulfilled. It can be the wry smile of a restrained and therefore more believable approval, or the patient smile of someone being made fun of but willing to be the butt of the joke. Or it can be the smile that emanates from calm inner assurance and deep self-confidence, the smile of someone who knows that beauty is only canvas deep.

The *Mona Lisa* is a prime choice for advertisers because she is famously open to interpretation. This is ironic because advertisers are generally allergic to interpretation. They quest for clarity. They don't see any real value in being misunderstood and don't like to take the risk. Clear communication is their goal, not enigmatic evocation.

It is even more ironic that an icon of enigma has become a first choice for products that have everything to do with clarity. Advertisers of consumer electronics love *Mona*. They want to tell you how easily their software can manipulate her image, or how clearly their technology can replicate that image again and again with no loss of fidelity, or how perfectly they can reproduce the subtle colors of a brilliant masterpiece.

Because her smile is famous for being interpretable—it never looks the same twice—it lets these advertisers be entertainingly coy about what they are selling. They want you to know that they can give you a replica of her image so perfect and exact that it allows no argument. They want you to smile because the image itself happens to be famous for never being seen the same way twice, no matter how perfectly it is replicated.

The *Mona Lisa* is so famous, and so overused, that simply copying her pose can evoke the painting's power. Playing the masterpiece angle, Fuji encourages you to compete with Leonardo by creating your own "Mona Debbie." Cobra, the French perfume, simply had an illustrator change everything

Above: Being the most popular image of female beauty made *Mona* a prime candidate for anyone selling any product that depended on the quality of reproduction.

Art foe must **MEET** *with* **THUNDER KICK.**

功夫

**KUNG FU
KITCHEN**

new art space   3047 LARIMER

Above: Advertising in the tradition of Duchamp, a modern art gallery explains itself by telling what it thinks of the old masters.

The Gunsmith and the Lady

Once a great artist left his easel to plan the arsenals and siege guns of a mighty war. The man was Leonardo da Vinci—many-sided genius of the Middle Ages. His name will never die. His work lives on—not in guns and things of battle, but in the smile of a lovely lady, the Mona Lisa of the Louvre.

Over and over in our world's history the arts of peace have been abandoned to make way for the crafts of war. Something like this has happened to us in America. To soldiers, to civilians and also to Olin Industries. Like everyone else, we've had to lay aside the job of peace to speed the hour of victory and hurry the day when we can all go back to making things that folks can enjoy in security and peace.

All that Olin chemists, engineers, metallurgists and technicians have learned in peacetime ...and in wartime will go into the hopper. Out will come many things—roller skates for children; guns and ammunition for sportsmen; flashlights and batteries for everyone; brass, bronze and other alloy metals now needed by manufacturers to make the myriad commodities that help make living pleasant and profitable.

That's what we dream of. It's a hope we share with all and it's bound to come true.

OLIN INDUSTRIES, INC.
East Alton, Illinois

about the source except three elements that make *Mona* the easy-to-recognize model: the eyes looking slightly right, the oddly elongated neck, and the patently enigmatic smile.

A more evocative and subtle example is the portrait of Iman for the elegant "Got Milk" campaign. Posed with *Mona's* politely crossed hands and clothed in a contemporary version of *Mona's* dark shawl, she coyly lets us know that she was born "a long time ago." Her smile makes the point, although in this case the lovely milk mustache has nothing enigmatic about it.

Another reason *Mona* is so popular is that she allows advertisers to reference da Vinci, an artist so famous he is identified as easily by his first name as his last. Leonardo's fame as an engineer, inventor, and a scientist makes *Mona* fair game for a wider range of advertisers. She is not limited to products that have to do with women or with beauty or with sex or perfume, as is often the case with paintings famous for the beauty of their subjects.

Look, for instance, at how far afield *Mona* travels in "The Gunsmith and the Lady," a corporate ad that Olin ran in the 1940s. Here we see Leonardo painting *La Giaconda*. We are told that America and Olin are just like Leonardo. We have had to "lay aside the job of peace" to make the stuff of war. Olin scientists will put their knowledge to work in "wartime," but we should rest assured that soon enough the company will return to making the "myriad commodities that help make living pleasant and profitable."

A little more logical in the use of *Mona* to get to Leonardo is Fiat, which asks, "Did Leonardo Da Vinci Design the First Fiat?" (see page 65) Fiat, after all is "the finest blend of art and engineering." It reveals "the Italian eye for beautiful form." And the price, well, that's the *pièce de résistance* that actually brings "the famous smile" to *Mona's* face. And then, with the sort of indifference that plays so nicely to our stereo-

type of Italy as a place more devoted to beauty than to logic, the ad concludes less persuasively than it might. "Did Leonardo, indeed, dream the first Fiat? Who cares!" Happily driving away in her Fiat, *Mona* looks out at us with the smile that says she knows but isn't telling.

As a symbol of high art for the art world, and being used as a constant plaything of advertising, *Mona* was a perfect target when the worlds of high culture and consumer culture began to meld together in the pop art movement. Some of the ads here came before pop and some came after, but they all serve to mark the ever-provocative collision between high and low. Through the power of repetition, advertisers have managed to take the gold standard of Renaissance mastery and turn it into an image too common to notice—and then by persisting, to transport its value as art into a new value in a commodity culture. Once the art world's most famous object of desire, *La Giaconda* is now the marketplace's queen of kitsch, reigning not only from the pages of magazines but from towels, mugs, T-shirts, and wherever images can be sold.

And all the while that enigmatic smile makes you wonder if that is such a bad thing after all.

I have to admit—I was sort of born with this body. But that was a long time ago. And now I have to work hard to keep it up. So what do I recommend? Ice-cold skim milk. With nine essential nutrients and no fat, it's everything a woman could want. Well, that and a chance to meet my husband—I guess.

MILK
What a surprise!"

Opposite: *Mona Lisa's* popularity also made da Vinci available as an endorser of company's who wanted to use art to sell. This Olin ad from the 1940s compares Leonardo to Olin, and to America. Like Leonardo, Olin can create products for both peace and war.

Above: *Mona's* pose is so well known it offers the perfect framing to evoke Iman's classical beauty while putting her in the irreverent tradition of Duchamp's mustachio'd *Mona*.

DA VINCI WORKED IN OILS.
WE PREFER MUD.

FORD RANGER 4X4.

• HIGHEST QUALITY OF ANY DOMESTIC COMPACT PICKUP* • ELECTRONIC FUEL-INJEC
• 4-WHEEL ANTI-LOCK BRAKES • STANDARD DRIVER'S AIR BAG AND NEW AVAILABLE
AIR BAG** • SWITCH-ON FOUR-WHEEL DRIVE • SIX-DISC CD CHANGER† • REMOTE KEY

*Based on an average of consumer-reported problems at three months ownership in a survey of Ford and competitive models designed and built in No
†Feature optional. **Always wear your safety belt.

This Spread: Da Vinci's engineering skills are rarely evoked
without reference to *Mona*. In
these cases, her smile takes a
back seat to his role as the
supremely skilled creator.
Opposite: Fiat used da Vinci's
Mona by pointing not only to
da Vinci's sense of engineering
and sense of beauty, but also to his
good sense to be Italian in the first
place.

Did Leonardo Da Vinci Design the First Fiat?

Could be. Leonardo, as every schoolboy knows, was both artist and engineer. He anticipated the cantilever bridge, aircraft and submarines. Who's to say that the automobile escaped his inspired vision? Fiat is Italy's finest blend of art and engineering. The Italian eye for beautiful form is evident in the lively, young lines. And the Italian talent for engineering comes through when you zing through the streets and highways. Did someone mention money? This 600D is an incredible $1262.* (Perhaps that accounts for the famous smile on Leonardo's Mona Lisa!) No car at anywhere near its price is so alert and alive. The Fiat you buy is especially made for use in the U.S.A. And cared for by factory-trained specialists at 425 parts-and-service centers. Did Leonardo, indeed, dream the first Fiat? Who cares! *Always have at least one* **FIAT**

*Suggested price p.o.e. New York. See the Yellow Pages for your nearest Fiat dealer. Overseas delivery through dealers and travel agents, or write Fiat Motor Co., Inc., 500 Fifth Avenue, N.Y., N.Y. 10036

REC

New
Handycam
Stamina

Up to
15 hours
continuous
recording

"...the picture becomes more

wonderful to us than it really is,

and reveals to us a secret which,

in truth, it knows nothing..."

O S C A R   W I L D E

SONY

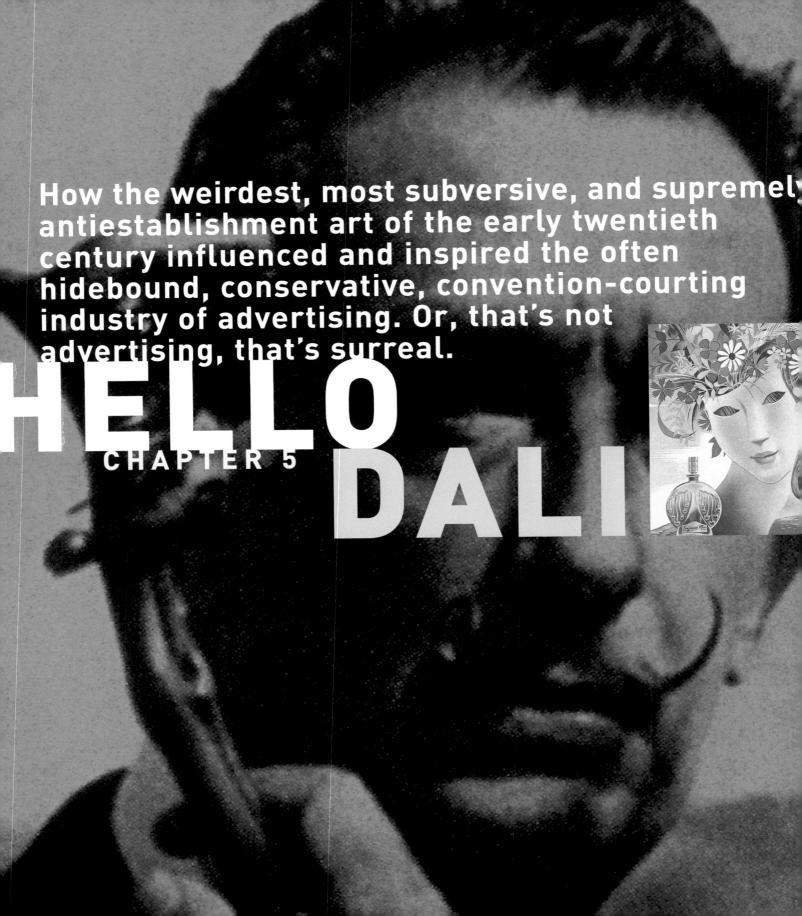

How the weirdest, most subversive, and supremel
antiestablishment art of the early twentieth
century influenced and inspired the often
hidebound, conservative, convention-courting
industry of advertising. Or, that's not
advertising, that's surreal.

HELLO
DALI

CHAPTER 5

"This rapid domestication of
the outrageous is the most
characteristic feature of our
artistic life . . ."

LEO STEINBERG

SURREAL
is a word heard as often on evening newscasts
as in art galleries and museums.

Surreal is a word heard as often on evening newscasts as in art galleries and museums. The surrealist movement may have run out of energy, but the work that it generated has come to define a way of explaining the world to a public who has very little idea of what surrealism was.

Surrealism had two practitioners whose thinking and work came to embody the movement. Marcel Duchamp stands as the most provocative and influential artist of the movement. Salvador Dali turned the movement into an industry and, more than anyone else, helped make the imagery of surrealism fodder for advertising.

Duchamp's stunning conceptualizations, his taunting ironies and oblique explorations, and his bad-boy subversiveness took on the institutions of the art world with a satirical wit so wry and deflating that it still turns heads a century later. There are few concepts with more resonance than the ready-made urinal Duchamp titled *Fountain,* signed with the punning alias "R. Mutt," and installed in a gallery as a work of art. While Duchamp's work represents some of the most provocative elements of the surrealist movement, Dali remains the most famous, the most commercial, and from the point of view of advertising, the most influential. Dali took the idea of surrealism and executed it with such abandon that he literally created an industry around himself. Today art expos sell every kind of reproduction of Dali's works, from oils to sculptures to tchotchkes. Indeed, the commercialization of

Dali's work illustrates why surrealism was so handily adapted to advertising. On the surface, the movement would seem too strange to offer anything to an endeavor that is by definition aimed at the widest audience available. What, after all, did advertising see in surrealism?

Dali and other surrealists manipulate and distort the mundane actuality of the world we live in to reveal the imagined world of our hidden desires. With different goals and different motives, this is exactly the conceptual space where advertising is often most at home. The curators at Tate Modern titled their 2002 show *Surrealism: Desire Unbound* and organized the hundreds of paintings, books, poems, photographs, and sculptures around the idea of desire. The choice of theme spells out why surrealism was so readily absorbed by advertisers in America.

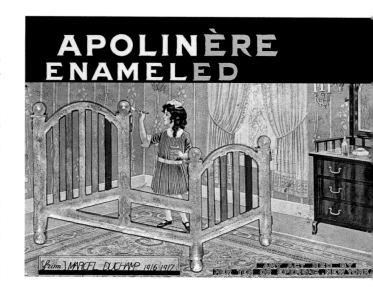

Above: Altering an ad painted on a tin sign, Duchamp dedicated it to fellow surrealist Guillaume Apollinaire. This "ready-made," like *The Fountain* and his defaced *Mona Lisa* postcard, define a world where art, manufactured goods, and advertising are used to blur and erase the boundaries between high culture and low.

Surrealist influence on advertising reached its greatest levels starting in the late 1930s and continuing through the early 1950s. That was a time when duty called, when repression was stronger than expression, when conformism was more powerful than individualism. Selling to a population that had been tempered by the Depression, burdened by the demands of mobilization and four years of world war, commercial interests might be expected to adopt public imagery that would be anything but adventurous and odd. And in many ways the advertising of that period is thoroughly conservative. The dominant advertising aesthetic of the period is probably best expressed by the likes of Maxfield Parrish and Norman Rockwell. Yet there was a parallel trend, a set of ads which have been mostly overlooked since they came and went in the marketplace, but which, in varying degrees, were influenced by surrealist painting.

Unlike the way they use classical painting, advertisers don't often reproduce the actual surrealist images. More often they transpose the visual rhetoric of surreal paintings with a glib indifference to the deeper issues and ideas that spawned the movement in the first place. Part of the comfort art directors felt when they presented surreal images to their clients must have sprung from the fact that surrealism, like advertising, is at its heart about desire.

IF SURREALISM IS ABOUT DESIRE UNBOUND,
THEN ADVERTISING IS ABOUT DESIRE BOUND.

Following Spread (left): Hanes uses a surreal landscape and a bizarre portrait of one woman's unconscious yearnings for another to sell the sexiness of seamless nylons.
Following Spread (right): Commissioned by Datsun, Dali renders a driverless car moving through a timescape while naked figures dance, joust, paint, and play.

To Grand Expectations.

The motives couldn't be more contrary,
the goals couldn't be more at odds, but the matter is the same. It is the essential sexuality of the surrealists that made the movement such a rich source for advertisers of products whose appeal was essentially sexual.

Happiness bestowed by attractiveness, beauty, and good looks is one of advertising's major preoccupations. A surrealistic style is well suited to the selling of cosmetics, where enticement is about image and gesture. Before photography became the dominant means of portraying beauty, art directors turned to painters and illustrators to tap into deep and unspoken feelings. Surrealist images showed a reality distorted by desire. The surrealists found ways to portray a world where reality was recognizable—unlike the cubists, for instance—but dreamlike, a world where boundaries were drawn from the dreaming mind more than the conscious mind. For the surrealists, desire at its core is about eroticism and individual freedom, about unshackling your mind from the constraint of middle-class conformity. Advertising, on the other hand, is an engine that works to have it both ways— making you feel like you are exercising your freedom as an individual while encouraging you to make the same choice as everyone else. What could be better than a million individ-

uals choosing to satisfy their desires in the same way and still feeling respected as individuals? When Dali wrote in 1931, "The culture of the mind will become identified with the culture of desire," he wasn't necessarily thinking of advertising, but thanks to modern marketing that is exactly what has happened.

Surrealism is the avant-garde, advertising the rear guard. Surrealists wanted more freedom than society would allow and used art to break down the intellectual barricades wherever they found them—and they found them everywhere. America wanted a society based on as much commercial freedom as could be allowed, with as little sexual freedom as could be tolerated.

Opposite and Above: The spirit of Grand Marnier's surreal ads is rooted in the work of René Magritte. But fellow surrealist Paul Delvaux's *The Break of Day* is also a direct source. For current sites on surrealism try **surrealism.nl, supervert.com** and **bongliquid.com. usc.edu** has a list of related Dali links. **massurrealism.com** gives you a view of surrealism today.

The revolution the surrealists argued for finally came to pass after the Second World War and the recovery that occurred in the 1950s. By the 1960s the repressive social order the surrealists had fought to destroy was collapsing under the sheer demographic force of the baby boomers, who took hold of the commercial culture's imagination and have yet to let go.

Indeed, the baby-boom generation was an object of desire so attractive to advertisers that they began to use sex with less restraint than ever before. Rarely a leader in anything, advertising followed shifts in the culture closely, codifying them as soon as they appeared safe for business. When it came to the public display of sex, film took the lead. Pornography became a multibillion-dollar business. Mainstream films became so daring, they inspired a rating system. Television, the medium most dependent on advertising, remained the most conservative until the advent of cable, when the broad audience could be parsed and its particular desires addressed to any advertiser's satisfaction.

As we look backward, there is no better place to peg the beginning of this huge cultural shift than in the philosophy and paintings of the surrealists. They, more than any other group, created the psychosocial vocabulary that the modern media use to engage us in stories and to sell us products. It's hardly surprising, since the surrealists were themselves a multimedia movement. From novels to poems to sculpture to theatre sets and movies like *Un Chien andalou*, they worked tirelessly to engage the largest public possible. The arenas of desire they first brought into public view we now take for granted. And we can trace their legacy in the advertising they influenced over the decades.

Opposite and Above: The simple visual tactics of distortion and juxtaposition are motivated by a belief that the actual world is more vivid when perceived through the lens of the unconscious. Advertisers saw surrealist techniques as a provocative means to get the attention of their customers, whether they were selling perfume or batteries.

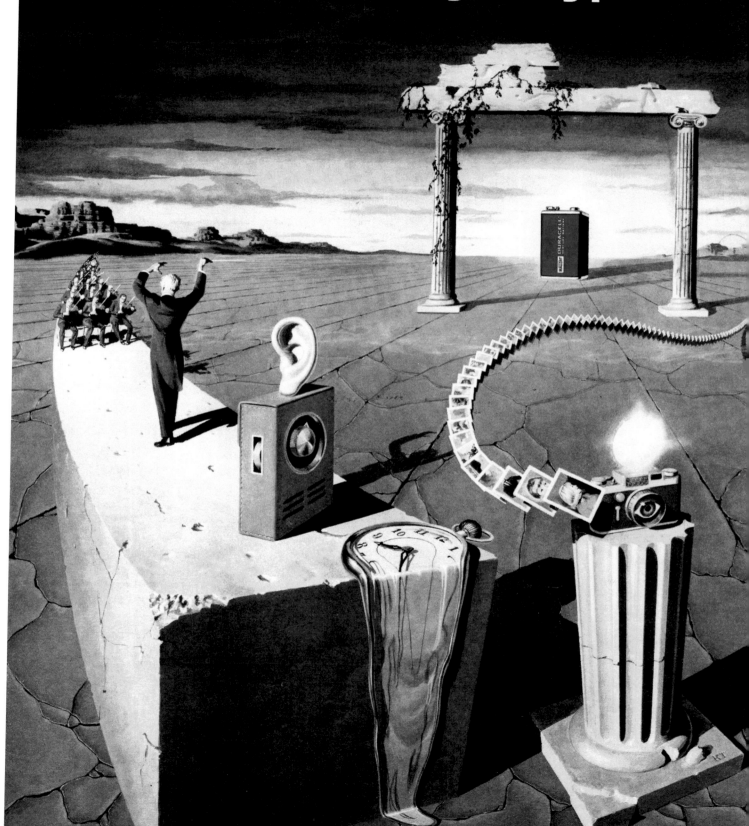

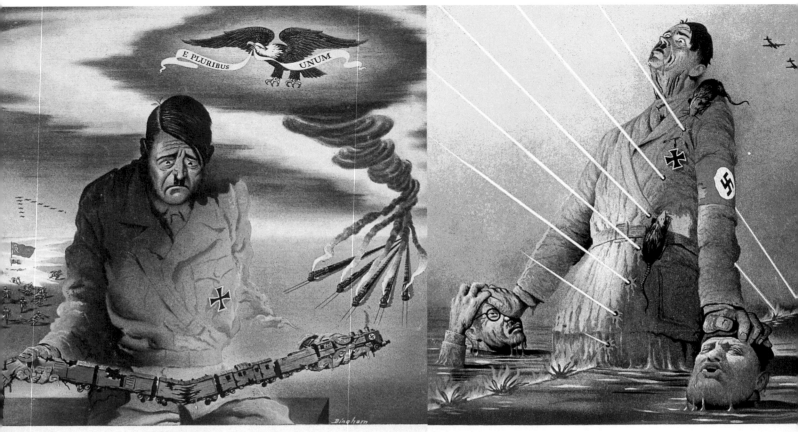

Railroads *made Hitler*

the sick man of Europe

HIS RAILROADS . . . AND OURS.   **HIS** because he neglected them . . . caused the railroad break-down inside Europe, first of the internal German collapses the civilized world longs to see.   **OURS** because American railroad men, handling history's greatest traffic with fewer cars and engines, *are the miracle men Hitler would have liked his Germans to be.*   Koppers, making many railroad products last much longer, saves railroads hundreds of thousands of priceless man-hours.   *Example:* Locomotives once were laid up every 25,000-45,000 miles for new piston packing. Now locomotives having Koppers American Hammered packing average 100,000 miles, and have hit a quarter million.   *Example:* Railroads once tore up millions and millions of ties a year. *Decay!* Now pressure-creosoted ties last 20-30 years instead of 5-6.   *Example:* Railroads own 370,000 buildings. Koppers coal-tar materials keep maintenance effort at a minimum on the roofs of thousands of these.— Koppers Company, Pittsburgh, Pa.

Buy United States War Bonds and Stamps

KOPPERS
THE INDUSTRY THAT SERVES ALL INDUSTRY

OIL

is dandy
for
drowning

Greatest mystery of the war: "Where is the Luftwaffe?"   Auth has plenty of oil . . . BUT hasn't plenty of 100-octane gas. Mar to use 60-octane.   A neat little partnership of oil and coal i position on 100-octane.   To make, entirely from oil, the qua fuel that American fighters need would have gobbled up enormous metals. That's where coal came in.   Coal is coked in Koppers recover much benzene. Combine benzene with propylene (an oil re you get a compound with an octane blending rating of 132 and other in aviation fuel. Americans add this to gasoline of say 70-octane a mixture up to around 100.

Koppers also furnishes to the oil industry: plants for purifying gas . . . piston rings . . . self-aligning couplings . . . pressure-treated timbers, and other products.—Koppers Company and Affiliates, Pittsburgh, Pa.

Buy United States Wa

KOPP
THE INDUSTRY THAT S

Above: The popularity of surreal imagery even made it appropriate for manufacturers. Koppers was a mainstay of America's heartland coal and steel industry during the war. Touting their contribution, the otherwise conservative managers were inspired to let their unconscious desires loose on Hitler himself.

Salvador Dali wore khakis.

**New Datsun 610 Wagon.
An original portrait by Salvador Dali.**

Own a Datsun Original.

Above: Dali's *Persistence of Memory* was widely imitated, even by Dali himself. The timescape he painted for Datsun, with naked figures dancing, is as idiosyncratic as car ads get. Dali also worked as an endorser. Surrealistically appropriate, Gap exumed his image from the grave to hawk khakis.

SPECTACULAR SHEERNESS

in Autumn's own color harmonies:

VERDÉ, POMMARD, MESA GREY, ALLSPICE,
COFFEE BEAN, MIMI, MILADY, CAFÉ AND
TERRA-COTTA (shown) . . .
54-60-66 gauge . . . 15 Denier

BEAUTIFUL
Bryans

Opposite: Dali's rendition of
autumn for Bryan's hosiery turns
ballerinas into dandelions, in a
world where gems, clouds,
cherubs, and ants are all

inspired to joyful dancing.
Above: Surreal imagery in
advertising is often burdened
by the weight of literalness.
This moisturizer ad tries to evoke

the belief that the disembodied
hand of a suitor will caress the
arm of his disembodied lover
despite existing in a world where
only a cactus could thrive.

80 81
Chapter 5 / HELLO DALI

A Chicago paper company becomes the preeminent patron of art in advertising and brings Bauhaus design to the American scene. All the while fighting Hitler, touting world peace and giving the likes of de Kooning, Cornell, Léger, Jacob Lawrence, and René Magritte a chance to sell some empty cardboard boxes.

CHAPTER 6

THE PATRON AND THE PACKAGE

"Advertising is the very essence of democracy."
BRUCE BARTON

"The one thing about commercial illustration, even at the highest level, is that the destination is handed to the illustrator before he sets off...In contrast, the fine artist begins his work to discover his destination."
ALAN MAGEE

"You can tell the ideals of a nation by its advertisements."
NORMAN DOUGLAS

Cosimo de Medici, Pope Julius II, and Walter Paepcke all had one thing in common. They were patrons of the arts, and they used the art they patronized to enhance themselves and the institutions they represented. Julius made himself immortal by commissioning the Sistine Chapel. The Medici gave their name and the city-states they ran a purchase on immortality by hiring the likes of Botticelli, Michelangelo, and Bronzino to paint their portraits and express their values.

Walter Paepcke is not quite so well known. He wasn't God's vicar on earth. He didn't prevail over the richest domain of the Renaissance. But like the Medici and the pope, he understood that art, and the ideas it expressed, could set the institution he led apart from the competition.

As chairman of the Container Corporation of America, in the 1940s and 1950s Paepcke transformed the company into a patron of the arts. Prompted and guided by his wife, Elizabeth, he commissioned painters and other artists from around the world to create ads for his enterprise. Under his leadership CCA became the first corporation in modern times to act not only as a purveyor in a market economy but as a patron in a cultural landscape.

The Paepckes were part of the intellectual society surrounding Robert Hutchins's University of Chicago. Along with Hutchins, Mortimer Adler, and others, they helped create the Aspen Institute, a retreat where the intellectual shakers of the academic world hobnobbed with the more pragmatic movers of the business world. But the Aspen Institute was only a logical extension of the Paepckes' commitment to the arts and to finding a way to integrate them into the culture at large.

The source of their money was a company that made cardboard. And while their commitment to art was personal and philosophical, it was still the case that their business did have something to do with design and imagery. Packaging and package design were as important a part of the growth of commodity culture as print ads, billboards, and radio commercials. Anything that encouraged people to think about packaging was going to be good for anyone in the paper products business, let alone the Container Corporation of America, which was one of the country's premier paper goods manufacturers.

But Paepcke's motives were not merely to sell the boxes CCA actually made. He saw advertising as a forum for the values of art. In this sense he prefigures Michel Roux, who brought commissioned artists to the Absolut Vodka campaign.

Paepcke's goal in commissioning his artists was much less marketing-driven than Barratt's was in his seminal Pears' soap campaign. Paepcke hoped his campaign would do well, but his goal was to do good. Living through the Depression and the devastation of Hitler's genocidal war had given him a desire to promote unity over sales. He wanted to heal the rift that in his view had developed between the low-culture world of business and the high-culture world of art.

"During the last century," he wrote, mass production had brought about an "unfortunate divergence in work and philosophy of the industrial producer and the artist." Yet, he believed artists and businessmen "have much in common and can contribute the more to society as they come to complement their talents." He saw in democratic America a place where the spirit of art and the values of business might easily enhance each other. Paepcke had a humanist's utopian instinct in him. He envisioned a world where artists and businessmen would both benefit by acknowledging what they had in common and ignoring what kept them apart.

Whether artist or businessman, "each has within him the undying desire to create, to contribute something to the world, to leave his mark on society; each has the necessity to earn and provide a living for himself and his family." The businessman trying hard to be a provider has neglected the creative side of his nature. The artist, seeming to create in a "vacuum," can't "provide."

Opposite: Early CCA ads used Bauhaus refugees such as Herbert Bayer to extol the contribution paper boxes were making to the American economy.

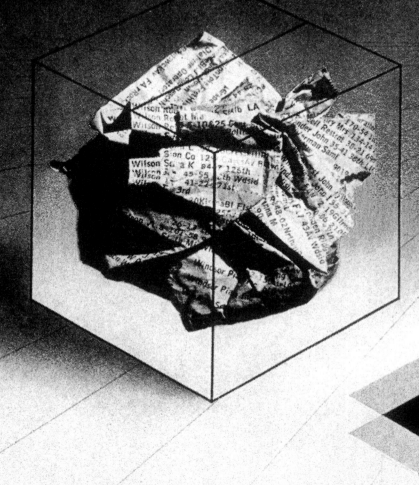

Destiny of an old Directory

Used paper of all kinds is reclaimed—4,000,000 tons a year—
as raw material for America's giant paperboard industry!

CONTAINER CORPORATION OF AMERICA

Paepcke's remedy is to overcome the divide. "Closer cooperation and understanding should help the businessman to produce material things which are not only functional and mechanically sound, but also artistically outstanding, and the artist in turn to share to a greater extent in the earning possibilities which are essential for a happy existence."

This union of art and business was, in Paepcke's view, a remedy to the situation of a world at war. "The artist and the businessman should cultivate every opportunity to teach and supplement one another, to cooperate with one another, just as the nations of the world must do. Only in such a fusion of talents, abilities, and philosophies can there be even a modest hope for the future, a partial alleviation of the chaos and misunderstandings of today,

AND A FIRST SMALL STEP TOWARD A GOLDEN AGE OF TOMORROW."

This is American optimism with a vengeance, rooted in the European dream of a New World, all the more vivid in the face of the Old World destroyed. The notion (prompted by Elizabeth— daughter of a University of Chicago professor) that advertising for cardboard boxes is one small step on the road to the "Golden Age of Tomorrow" is a measure of Paepcke's hopefulness, his depth of belief in the promise of the American experiment.

In CCA ads, for the first time, ideas and images took precedence over product. They said more about who the company was than about what it made. The ads looked different, and the effect of that aesthetic difference was noticeable in business. Paepcke wrote that "the direct sale of boxes is not and never has been the purpose of our institutional advertising. But, insofar as it creates an acute awareness of our company, giving it a distinctive personality and identifying it with the best in graphic art, it succeeds extremely well."

Paepcke, his director of advertising Egbert Jacobson (a former art director at J. Walter Thompson), and Charles Coiner, the art director at N. W. Ayer in charge of the project, started out giving work to artists and designers who had fled Hitler. In the avant-garde world of European design, these artists had already chalked up considerable careers at the Bauhaus, among such influential figures as Paul Klee, Wassily Kandinsky, Josef Albers, Laszlo Moholy-Nagy, Ludwig Mies van der Rohe, and Walter Gropius.

As Michele Bogart points out in her thorough and invaluable look at the relationship between fine and commercial art in twentieth-century America, these men created advertising that bore little or no resemblance to the commercial work of the day.

Daniel Catton Rich, the director of the Art Institute of Chicago, noted as much after he mounted an exhibition of eighty-nine ads in 1946. He said he was disappointed because,

Paepke's commitment to the idea that fine art and design could distinguish a corporation

created numerous followers. Dole Pineapple enlisted Georgia O'Keefe and A.M. Cassandre,

while others from Pepsi-Cola to Lucky Strikes commissioned fine artists to help them sell.

together, none of the work had the startling effect they had had when he had seen them in *Fortune, Time,* and *Business Week.* In his museum they were all, more or less, examples of modernism, while in their original venues they had starkly defined just how traditional the advertising that surrounded them was. But taken in context or out, they remain a remarkable collection.

When it began in May of 1937, the campaign was a revelation. It followed principles of design and composition that put the integration of type and visual elements at a premium. Those principals guided the evolution of the campaign over four decades, as it moved from topic to topic. In the '30s the topics were the cardboard box and the company. In the '40s the ads focused on the box and America's role as a supplier to the Allies. In the '50s Paepke initiated the *Great Ideas of Western Man* series. The campaign also honored every state of the union by commissioning a local artist to execute an ad honoring his state.

Throughout all the changes, the campaign maintained an attitude of unalloyed sincerity. There is not a shred of irony. This is not the Dada school of subversive culture-crossing. It is not the pop school of self-referential coolness. It is rather a world of high-minded ideals.

The evolution of subject matter itself is interesting to follow, if only because it seems prompted less by the demands of business and sales and more by changes in geopolitics. But whatever CCA chose to focus on, it always gave the artists the freedom to do what they wanted, as long as it was sincere. "We have never given them any instructions or directions," Herbert Bayer wrote. "All we have asked is that the artist do something which he feels is an interpretation of the quotation. . . . The company has done nothing more than accept or reject the product. What you see is a true and unfettered expression of the artists' own feelings, with no influence . . . whatsoever."

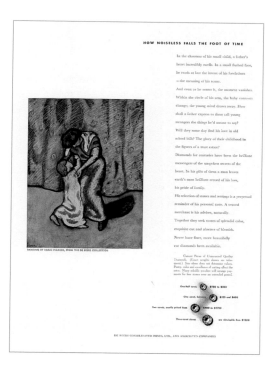

Above: A work of art, like a diamond, is forever. De Beers used Picasso, Dali, and others to associate their diamonds with the timeless, priceless qualities of fine art. Like CCA, De Beers used art to distinguish its image.

In the beginning, the corporation gave their artists subjects that were slightly less abstract than they were later to become. The artists received what Herbert Bayer described as "simple statements about the company, its operations, products, materials, resources, its contributions to the national economy." The only limitation was that the headline, such as it was, could never be longer than fifteen words. A partial list of the subjects for the first ten years of ads illustrates just how simple and pointed the campaign was in its beginning.

U.S. weapons and food are being sent to the Russian front in paper packages. 4,000,000 tons of newspaper and office wastepaper a year is recycled. We make boxes out of 17,000,000 bales of wheat. The army eats powdered eggs delivered in paper containers. We produce more weapons because packages that used to be made of metal are now made of cardboard. War materiel travels to the front in boxes. We're learning new skills in wartime. What's the process of making paper? We've got allies. We're first in research. We're diversified. We invest in research. Paper is not just strong it's also beautiful. Versatility is a good thing. Concentrating is a good thing. Unity is a good thing. An integrated company is a good thing. The United Nations is a good thing. We work in Latin America. We send things to Poland in boxes. World trade is a good thing. Anti-communist guerrillas get their weapons in paper packages. Yugoslavian patriots get supplies in our boxes. Taking responsibility is a good thing. Our boxes are strong. So is our company. We know what we're doing. Paper boxes help consumers get a fair shake. Paperboard helps feed the starving children of India. Gasoline can travel in boxes. We support the resistance by parachuting supplies in boxes. Paper boxes are watertight. Stability is a good thing. Harmony is a good thing.

Opposite: Willem de Kooning took the CCA assignment and created a simple scene of his fellow countryman working on the docks in Holland, enjoying the value of Paepke's containers as tools for gaining "liberation."

U. S. supplies, packed in paper, speed the liberation of The Netherlands and colonies

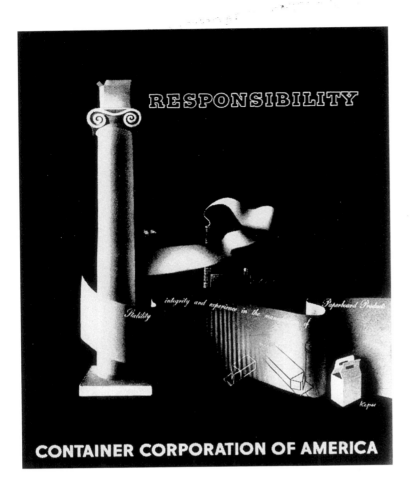

RESPONSIBILITY

Stability   *integrity and experience in the m...*   *Paperboard Product*

Kepes

CONTAINER CORPORATION OF AMERICA

The solutions generated by artists in response to these ideas integrated text with design in ways that no one had seen before, and in ways that still stand out today. They expressed the basic Bauhaus notion that in an industrial society, form follows function and there is precious little room for decoration. The symbolic impact of the graphic matters more than the pictorial power of the image. Abstraction, married with explicit, brief, staccato language, is seen as the best way to make the point. There are no long paragraphs explaining what you see. The CCA campaign is still a graphic benchmark that became the seed for some of the best graphic design we see today.

Two influential artists who did some of the most distinctive early work for CCA were Gyorgy Kepes and Herbert Bayer. Kepes, who fled the Nazis, arrived in the United States in the late '30s and was immediately given work on the Container Corporation of America's campaign. Having come under the influence of Gropius at the Bauhaus, he devoted the rest of his life to bridging the gap between the arts and industry, between imagination and technology. Gropius wanted a world "without the class-distinctions that raise an arrogant barrier between craftsmen and artists." Once that barrier is down, a society built upon this philosophy "will one day rise towards the heavens from the hands of a million workers as the crystalline symbol of a new and coming faith." In Gropius's manifesto we can see an early version of the way Paepcke thought about his hiring of artists and graphic designers to do his advertising.

And we see the ideas that Kepes spent the rest of his life studying, writing about, and visually expressing. He too wanted to break down the barrier between the businessman and artist as a means to resurrecting the Golden Age. Upon his death, at ninety-five, in December of 2001, Kepes was described as "the greatest pioneer in the marriage of art and technology in America, if not the world. He was a visionary,

Above: Gyorgy Kepes integrated type and images to create a design tableaux of didactic symbols—columns, paper, boxes—to present the abstract corporate virtues that CCA wanted to express.

a towering intellect, and a breathtaking artist. He single-handedly created the Center for Advanced Visual Studies at MIT and turned it into an internationally acclaimed program for the development of the finest in late twentieth-century art." That career began in America with his work for CCA.

Herbert Bayer, who died in 1985, was also a student at the Bauhaus, where he studied with Wassily Kandinsky. An Austrian by birth, Bayer fled Germany in 1938. Like Kepes, in much of his work he followed the mantra proclaimed by Gropius: "art and technology—a new unity." The same mantra motivated Paepcke not only in his advertising campaign but in his funding of the Institute of Design in Chicago (where Laszlo Moholy-Nagy, the director, always had a place for fellow Bauhaus exiles) and the Aspen Institute. Like Kepes and Paepcke, whether working in photography, paint, photomontage, sculpture, or architecture, Bayer always explored ways to bring the values of art and of modern industrial society (see page 85) into closer alignment.

Given who they were and where they came from, it's clear why Paepcke was eager to enlist these young men in the service of advertising his corporation. The results are classics of design that have influenced generations of art directors and designers.

David Ogilvy, the founder of Ogilvy & Mather (and, in company with Bill Bernbach and Rosser Reeves, part of the advertising equivalent of the Three Tenors), has had mixed feelings about the CCA campaign. "I denounced the campaign as an exercise in amateurish pretension. I pointed out that it violated all the principles of good advertising. . . . And I predicted that it would soon be consigned to oblivion. . . . Thirty-eight years have passed, and . . . I have come to think that it is the best campaign of corporate advertising that has ever appeared in print." On the other hand, he hastens to add, "I must admit that I have yet to read the copy in a Container Corporation advertisement, and in this I may not be alone: like many businessmen I have little interest in philosophy." Ogilvy simply admires the ads because they look so different, are consistent over the years, and have served to make the employees proud to be part of the company. Not to mention that, having grown the revenues of the company from very little to a billion dollars, they haven't embarrassed the shareholders. It is one of the few examples where high art, high ideals, and high profits have kept good company.

Just a small sampling of the two hundred ads from the last twenty years of the campaign can give a visceral sense of their difference, provocative impact, dignity, and scope. Over the years Paepcke called on many artists, from Willem de Kooning and Henry Moore to Joseph Cornell, Jacob Lawrence, René Magritte, and James Rosenquist.

It is not until the Absolut campaign of the 1980s that we will again see such a sophisticated, consistent, imaginative, and persistently provocative use of art in advertising.

GREAT IDEAS OF WESTERN MAN . . . one of a series

THEODORE ROOSEVELT on the preservation of America

The things that will destroy America are prosperity at any price, peace at any price, safety first instead of duty first, and love of soft living and the get-rich-quick theory of life.

(Letter to S. Stanwood Menken, January 10, 1917)
From "The Letters of Theodore Roosevelt," Harvard University Press

Payola

op Corruption Pre

Peddle

CONTAINER CORPORATION OF AMERICA   CCA

FRANCE REBORN *New lifeblood—supplies in paper packages.*

CONTAINER CORPORATION OF AMERICA

SAVE WASTE PAPER

Opposite: Bayer did this collage in the middle '50s. The ideas that became the stuff of the pop movement were already in the air. Compare this to Richard Hamilton's work on page 98.
Above: Fernand Léger, who found advertising images exciting, signed on to portray the joy of France at the end of World War II.

that margin between that which men naturally do and that which they can do is so great
that a system which urges men to action and develops individual enterprise and initiative is preferable
in spite of the wastes that necessarily attend that process

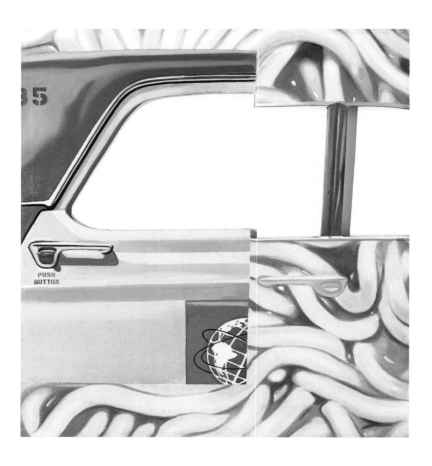

louis d. brandeis on democracy
artist: james rosenquist
great ideas of western man   one of a series

container corporation of america

Above: James Rosenquist, who once made his living painting billboards, was an appropriate choice to make us see the relationship between entrepreneur- ial potential and the risk of waste associated with consumerism.

Opposite (top left): Magritte managed a French advertising agency. His response to the quo- tation he was handed is one of the more direct and communica- tive of the "Great Ideas" series.

Opposite (top right): Joseph Cornell's boxes are the perfect

those who cannot remember the past   are condemned to repeat it

george santayana, the life of reason,
great ideas of western man... one of a series
container corporation of america

Carl Schurz on idealism

Ideals are like stars you will not succeed in touching them with your hands. But like the seafaring man on the desert of waters, you choose them as your guides, and following them you will reach your destiny. *Schurz, Faneuil Hall, Boston, April 18, 1859.*

Great Ideas of Western Man... one of a series   CONTAINER CORPORATION OF AMERICA

Great Ideas of Western Man... one of a series

Marcus Aurelius on brotherhood

Men exist for the sake of one another. Teach them then or bear with them.

CONTAINER CORPORATION OF AMERICA

American foods in paper packages aid Britain.

CONTAINER CORPORATION OF AMERICA

fit for an advertisement about idealism for a company that makes boxes.
Above (left): Jacob Lawrence, who chronicled African-

American life on canvas, contributed to CCA's campaign, portraying the concept of social responsibility.
Above (right): Known as a

sculptor more than a painter, Henry Moore's evocation of refugees sustaining themselves with the proceeds of American supplies is one of the most

touching of the CCA wartime series.

Tables are turned, products become art, critics go nuts, painters become celebrities, abstraction gets real, America laughs, and a white-haired illustrator named Andy turns himself into a brand that any advertiser would envy.

POP GOES THE EASEL

CHAPTER 7

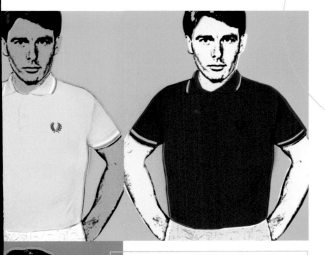

"Pop art counters abstraction with realism, the emotional with the intellectual, and spontaneity with conceptual strategy."

T I L M A N   O S T E R W O R L D

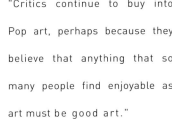

"Critics continue to buy into Pop art, perhaps because they believe that anything that so many people find enjoyable as art must be good art."

J E D   P E R L

CAN'T IGNORE POP

democratic-commercial-vulgar-kitschy-campy flux

Any look at the intersection of high culture and low, of masterpiece and mass reproduction, of beauty and persuasion, can't ignore pop. It occupies the space where art and advertising finally come together in a vast, churning, democratic-commercial-vulgar-kitschy-campy flux.

Pop uses advertising the same way it uses just about everything else in the culture. Comics and newspapers, toothpaste tubes and beer cans, soups and sodas, Marilyns and Maos become the subjects of art just as Madonnas and Medici were the apples of the eyes of every Renaissance practitioner worthy of a brush.

Richard Hamilton's list of the attributes of pop art reads like an advertising account executive's attempt to delineate a product's "brand essence." According to Hamilton pop is

POPULAR

TRANSIENT

EXPENDABLE

LOW COST

MASS PRODUCED

YOUNG

BIG BUSINESS

WITTY   GIMMICKY

GLAMOROUS

SEXY

Hamilton's list of attributes for the new art form he was practicing defines just as well the attributes of advertising as we have come to know them.

The seeds of pop blew in on many different cultural winds; as David McCarthy notes, it was the "son of Dada and Surrealism without the politics and without the attitude." Proponents pointed to its art historical lineage in order to claim for pop a legitimacy its critics never wanted to grant. The strong critical aversion to pop wasn't hard to explain. Pop got the short end of the critical stick because it accepted anything that commercial culture spawned.

Above: Richard Hamilton's 1956 collage of products, logos, and images lifted from magazines took as its title a coyly ironic question: *Just What is It that Makes Today's Homes So Different, So Appealing?* With John Ruskin's portrait looking on as the ghost of art history past, this room/world contains much of pop culture to come: sex, convenience, mass communications, narcissism, sentimentality, and abundance.

From the moment Lawrence Alloway named it in 1958, pop was fuel for argument. And while contending camps in art criticism either embraced or lambasted the movement, all in all the mass media were happy to cover it. The art was simple. It was pictures of things people knew and understood. It made for good copy.

When it came to the austere color fields of the minimalists or the which-way-is-up canvases of the abstract expressionists, the public at large could easily join in with Tom Wolfe's jaunty attack in *The Painted Word,* and thumb their noses at all that supposed meaning they weren't comprehending. With pop, however, they could at least appreciate the value of a soup can, a comic book, or a toothbrush. The works were fun. And whatever you might say they meant, at least you knew what you were looking at.

Originating in London in the late '50s, pop took hold in America and became known as an American movement. Its best known practitioners all started out in the pragmatic world of commercial art. Warhol, who came to New York from the art program at Carnegie Mellon in Pittsburgh, was thrilled to be designing shoe ads for Bonwit Teller. James Rosenquist painted billboards for the General Outdoor Advertising Company, Robert Rauschenberg was a commercial artist, and Roy Lichtenstein decorated windows.

They took their skills and their subjects and switched from being vendors to being producers. Instead of taking on assignments and getting paid to create a picture that enhanced the value of a product, they chose a product, an object, or an image they wanted to paint, and hoped that people would pay them for their point of view. Pop eliminates the middleman.

Above: Warhol exhibited his 32 soup cans in 1962 in Los Angeles. By mass producing in paint a brand image, he held a mirror up to the shifting border between commercial art and high art. It was a line that he and the other pop artists continued to explore.

Pop, like advertising, is interested in the concept more than the rendering. It uses the objects that inhabit the world every individual of every class takes for granted—the mundane, mass-produced stuff that is all around us. The things you use and like. Pop artists don't use these things because there is nothing else to paint; they use them to make a point.

Pop thumbed its nose at high culture (always mindful to be coy without being too angry or cutting), made fun of museums (while courting their recognition), and did what it could to accomplish what high art had always taken as *its* mission—to give us new ways to understand our world by giving us new ways to see it. Like advertising at its best, pop worked best when it gave us a dazzling glimpse of the obvious. His art, Jasper Johns said, "focused on things which are seen and not looked at." As Andy Warhol told *Time* in 1962, "I just paint things . . . you use everyday and never think about it."

Pop signaled the total triumph of the selling state of mind in American culture. It came after the world had left the devastation of the Second World War behind. After fifteen years of relative peace and prosperity, citizens had begun to see themselves as consumers. National and ethnic and regional identities were no longer the only way to understand your place in the world. The country was starting to understand itself in terms of demographics.

America had become a consumer society, a society that allowed you to express yourself freely by buying things you liked. The liberty to shop in the pursuit of happiness, as it turned out, was what we had fought a war to preserve. Democracy may be the most inefficient form of government, but it allowed for a great deal of efficiency when it came to producing things people wanted.

While critics, intellectuals, moralists, and spiritual mentors of every pulpit at times inveighed against materialism, capitalism, corporatism, and Mammon, consumerism barreled forward. It made life easier, simpler, more entertaining, and more convenient for more people in less time than any other movement had ever promised, let alone accomplished. It was democracy with a sales tag, and the sheer abundance of possibilities made the world feel open and egalitarian and hopeful.

Pop was the cave painting of this newly flush consumer ethic, and the success of pop artists was the high culture's acknowledgment of the irrefutable, unavoidable fact of these vast social changes. The critics who didn't like pop actually seemed to hate it, perhaps because pop signaled the complete collapse of the established standards in art and looked to them like a betrayal by members of their own class.

From Lawrence Alloway's influential point of view, pop was in the avant-garde tradition of articulating a new audience to itself. Pop represented the new hierarchy of power—the power of consumers. And once they saw pop, people liked it. Popularity is the free market's form of commission.

The Church of Rome in its heyday commissioned portraits of its saints and stories; the aristocratic classes of Europe commissioned portraits of their finery and fettle, and tableaux of their heroic exploits; the burghers of Holland encouraged family portraits to ennoble their newly accumulated wealth. But it wasn't until the middle of the twentieth century that the consumer class, in its own quest for recognition and identity, could find a means to express itself to itself, and to the world it was taking over. Pop was that means.

Modern art had cleared the way. The cubists and surrealists and the antics of the Dada coterie had made clear how dated all the previous hierarchies and orders and ways of seeing had become. But they had done it in the world of salons and galleries and museums. They had done it when art could still shock because it lived in a more cloistered world.

Pop spoke to a larger, more raucous world, for better and worse. By creating a visual and conceptual vernacular for

Opposite: Roy Lichtenstein did for comics and ads what Warhol did for cans and celebrities. By painting the Benday dots of printed material, he gave advertisers one of the few pop techniques they could borrow. Nivea, on the following spread, used it wittily to create a demonstration in print of how their cream can remove blackheads.

Clear-up Strip
removes blackheads

"What characterizes Pop is mainly its use of what is despised."
ROY LICHTENSTEIN

EN WHO DARE TO CARE

NIVEA
FOR MEN

its time, the movement made art interesting to the consuming class, not just to the class of people who consumed art. And it did so at a time when the consuming class was ready to see itself in all its ironic, materialist, self-satisfying, self-critical glory.

Instead of saints, there are superstars. Instead of portraits of merchants, there is merchandise. Instead of uniqueness and individuality, there are multiples and reproductions. Instead of sincerity, there is irony, indifference, and neutrality. Instead of a hostile distinction between advertising and art, there is a permeable membrane. Instead of cultural conflict between high and low, there is symbiosis.

"As an alternative to an aesthetic that isolated visual art from life and from the other arts," Alloway wrote in 1968, "there emerged a new willingness to treat our whole culture as if it were art. It was recognized in London for what it was ten years ago, a move toward an anthropological view of our society. The mass media were entering the work of art, and the whole environment was being regarded reciprocally by the artist as art, too."

Pop's willingness to be catholic about what it paints is at the crux of the violent critical reaction it provokes. There is a common thread of disdain for the subject matter pop chooses to give us dazzling glimpses of. As Hilton Kramer objected, "Pop Art does not tell us what it feels like to be living through the present moment of civilization—it's merely part of the evidence of that civilization. Its social effect is simply to reconcile us to a world of commodities, banalities, vulgarities, which is to say, an effect indistinguishable from advertising art."

Disturbed by pop's ease with advertising, the arbiters of taste are often reduced to ad hominem attacks, not only against the artists themselves but also against the audience that makes this banal art popular. Max Kozloff finds among pop artists "a curious, frank admission of chicanery . . . that does not necessarily succeed in seeming honest. . . Are we supposed to regard our popular signboard culture with more fondness now that we have Rosenquist? . . . The truth is, the art galleries are being invaded by the pinheaded and contemptible style of gum chewers, bobby soxers, and worse, delinquents." Referring to Warhol and others, Jules Langsner observes that pop suffers from a "poverty of visual invention. . . It is not the eye that is engaged but rather the play of ideas this genre generates whether one is looking at the work or not." Pop is conceptual; it operates by the same method as advertising at its best. Advertisers don't want you to study their technique or appreciate depth of meaning; they want to imprint a concept and a name on your memory. They want you to "get it" and to always see and think about their product whether you are looking at the ad or not.

Warhol often talked about his work with the same rhetoric you hear from advertising people. "Once you 'got' Pop, you could never see a sign the same way again. Once you thought Pop, you could never see America the same way again."

Warhol certainly saw himself as a man in the business of selling. While most of his interviews and writings have a curiously oblique quality to them, on the subject of the art of business and the business of art, he was positively lyrical.

This Spread: James Rosenquist juxtaposed images, objects, and ads. The technique gave the experience of flipping through a magazine. Simply by magnifying the images that fly by us every day, he gives us a reason to stop and consider how they are affecting us.

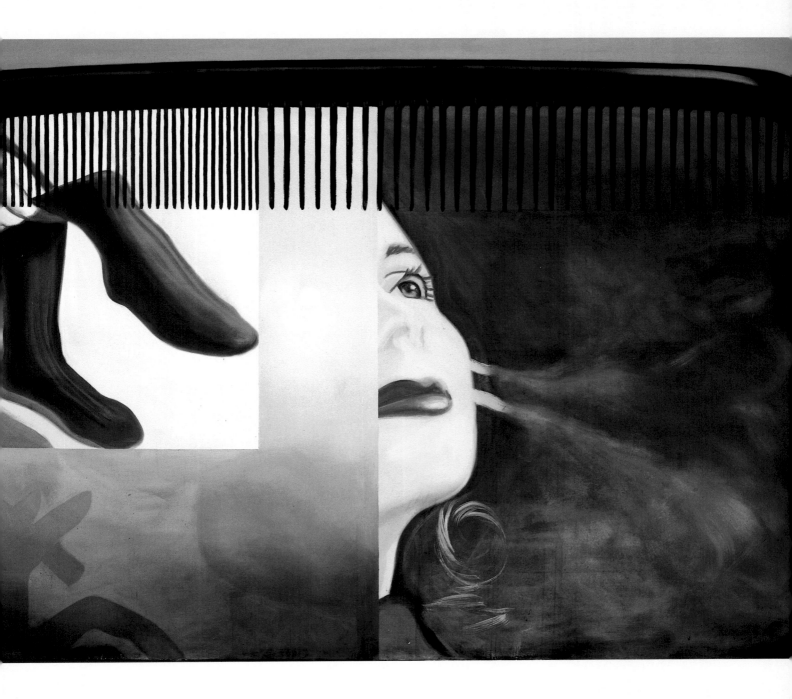

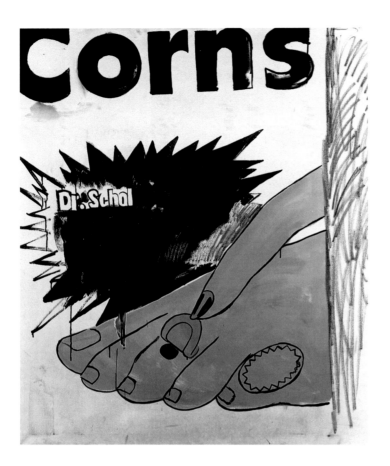

With his patented insouciance and studied naïveté, Warhol undercut his critics by agreeing with them. "Here I am," he said, "If you want to know all about Andy Warhol . . . just look at the surface of my paintings and films and me. There's nothing behind it." Warhol's subversiveness lay in being intellectually pesky and annoyingly vague. He presented himself as the man with the deepest shallows in America.

When Warhol first came to New York, he did shoe illustrations and did a lot of work for Bonwit Teller and *Glamour* magazine. "I loved working when I worked at commercial art and they told you what to do and how to do it and all you had to do was correct it and they'd say yes or no. The hard thing is when you have to dream up the tasteless things on your own."

Coming from commercial illustration, as he did, he had none of the disgust for the "wasteland" of kitsch that the critics of pop could not tolerate. In fact, where Alloway talked about commercial culture as the subject for art, Warhol saw business as an even higher form of self-expression. "Wasted space," he said perversely, "is any space that has art in it. An artist is somebody who produces things that people don't need to have but that he—for some reason—thinks it would be a good idea to give them.

"Business Art is a much better thing to be making than Art Art, because Art Art doesn't support the space it takes up, whereas Business Art does. (If Business Art doesn't support its own space it goes out of business.)"

Warhol's supposed goal in life was to move from being a commercial artist to being an artist to being a producer of art. He called his studio the Factory and was (for reasons as practical as they were aesthetic and philosophical) most interested in mass production and in whatever media came his way. His Factory, after all, didn't just produce silk screens but films and, of course, the magazine *Interview*.

He claims in his autobiographical *The Philosophy of Andy Warhol* to have been inspired (upon reading of Picasso's death) by the fact that Picasso had created four thousand masterpieces in his lifetime. "Gee, I could do that in a day," he thought to himself. He figured his silk-screen "technique" would allow him to produce four thousand identical masterpieces in a day. It turned out his technique wasn't up to the task and he could produce only five hundred in a month. So he stopped, disillusioned that the process would take so long.

Above: Warhol's early work began with the lowest of low culture. This is not Marilyn, Jackie O, Mona or Mao. By choosing to paint ads for corn removal, he was sure to get noticed by high-culture gatekeepers who were outraged by the vulgarity of pop's focus on mere consumer products.

As odd as such a moment is, it illustrates how pop made it hard to distinguish between high culture and low. The idea that a "masterpiece" could be endlessly replicated and still be the equivalent of Picasso's four thousand distinct "masterpieces," suggests how subversive to the aesthetics of high culture the pop program could be.

It is here that Warhol meets de Tocqueville. He sees the hierarchy of excellence dissolved by the excellence of egalitarianism. This is Warhol at his evocative, explanatory best.

"What's great about this country is that America started the tradition where the richest consumers buy essentially the same things as the poorest. You can be watching TV and see Coca-Cola and you can know that the President drinks Coke, Liz Taylor drinks Coke and just think, you can drink Coke too. A Coke is a Coke and no amount of money can get you a better Coke than the one the bum on the corner is drinking. All the Cokes are the same and all the Cokes are good. . . . All of this is really American. The idea of America is so wonderful because the more equal something is, the more American it is."

Warhol and most of the other pop artists express the conflict between freedom and egalitarianism that is at the political heart of the American experiment. Mass producers (and their advertising copywriters, art directors, and account executives) capitalized on that tension with increasing persistence and success as the century lumbered forward.

The pop project attacked high-culture elitism with abandon and assigned itself the job of creating the artists' chronicle of mass culture. As Oldenburg's manifesto manifests, they did so with gusto, embracing all criticism of banality by making banality the paradoxical point.

It was an embrace that made the high-culture gatekeepers increasingly annoyed. Peter Selz argued that the works of pop art ". . . share with all academic art—including by the

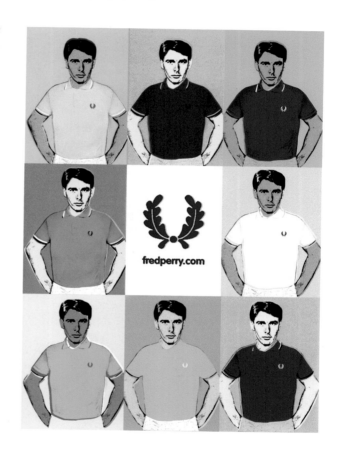

Above: Repetition of images distinguished pop art from art that honored the unique original. Fred Perry, a traditional English sportswear manufacturer angling for a youth-culture market, uses that tactic to present the variety of colors they carry while giving us a reason to believe that their shirts are hip.

WOW! WITH AS MUCH **CALCIUM** AS MILK, **NEW CALCIUM ENRICHED V8°** IS ALSO RICH IN **NUTRIENTS** LIKE **VITAMINS A** AND **C**, AND HAS THE **POTASSIUM** OF A **WHOLE BANANA!**

way Nazi and Soviet art—the refusal to question their complacent acquiescence to the values of the culture. And most ironic of all is the fact that this art of abject conformity, this extension of Madison Avenue, is presented as avant-garde. . . . It is as easy to consume as it is to produce and, better yet, is easy to market, because it is loud, it is clean, and you can be fashionable and at the same time know what you're looking at. . . . This is not a Folk art, grown from below, but kitsch, manufactured from above and given all the publicity Madison Avenue dealers have at their disposal." Pop is not only art about products in the marketplace, it is also a product in the marketplace of art. It seems that being more of the market than is allowed makes it correspondingly less artful.

In a sense, pop was the first truly popular, self-conscious foray of the high-art sensibility into the world of the selling culture. It was the canary in the mineshaft of consumerism that signaled, alarmingly to some, the recognition that the fine arts were no longer separate from the world of mass communication.

The shift was described by Raymond Williams from an economic and anthropological perspective. "Advertising," he argues, "is, in a sense, the official art of modern capitalist society; it is what 'we' put up in 'our' streets and use to fill up to half of 'our' newspapers and magazines, and it commands the services of perhaps the largest organized body of writers and 'artists,' with their attendant managers and advertisers, in the whole society."

Recognizing the dominant culture, pop gets its energy from the source and turns the no-man's-land between high art and low, between what Warhol calls Art Art and Business Art, into an all-men's-land, where ads are models for art, and art and ads are, if not indistinguishable, at least indivisible. Whether it's an ad, or a painting of an ad, it is part of the cult of likeability that has increasingly become the most valuable currency in advertising's bank of selling arguments.

This Spread: The popularity of Lichtenstein's Benday dots serves many masters. Sunlight uses them for a demonstration, just as Nivea did. Scoresby is content to play up the romantic subject matter Lichtenstein often highlighted. V8 goes directly for the comic book element so they can let the bottle sell us on its inner nutritional value. Visit **Lichtensteingallery.com** for more.

Watch a savvy Frenchman hire a shy Czech to paint a bottle of vodka and revive the role of art in advertising, while he leverages the power of demographics and reminds us of Cold War history, freedom, working stiffs, and the spirit of America's spirits.

ADVERTISING UNDER THE INFLUENCE

CHAPTER 8

"Making money is art and working is art and good business is the best art."

ANDY WARHOL

"Advertising is the greatest art form of the twentieth century."

MARSHALL McLUHAN

"Fun without sell gets nowhere but sell without fun tends to become obnoxious."

LEO BURNETT

HIS POWERFUL FUSION
OF ART AND ADVERTISING

Few categories of advertising have done more to leverage the various appeals of the fine arts in their selling arguments than liquor advertising.

You can occasionally see art put to use selling hops and brews, but in the land of beer advertising status is more often measured by the ability to impress women.

In beer advertising, "art" generally refers to expertise. Every now and then some import makes a point of talking about the "art" of brewing; Grölsch, for instance, is an import from Holland that has featured a painting of eighteenth-century burghers on its label. It positioned itself as the Dutch "masterpiece" of European brewing, taking a leaf from Dutch Coronas—the cigars that wanted us to believe that their quality was better because they came from a country where some people were particularly good painters.

Wine has used its fair share of artistic references as well. Coming to a parochial postwar America as the drink of France, with the associations of refinement, connoisseurship, and expertise, not to mention the café society of the Left Bank artists, wine has always used high culture references to distinguish its pedigree from the vulgarity of beer and hard liquor. Chateau Margaux gained wide notice when it hired Picasso and others to design its labels.

For the most part, however, it has been the hard liquors, both brown and white, that have appropriated high art to sell the product. One advertiser has developed a campaign and stuck with it for so long—twenty years and still going—that it alone has changed the boundaries between art and commerce.

The campaign for Absolut vodka has already inspired any number of books and enough rewards and recognition to fill a distillery. The Absolut Web site is devoted more to the arts than vodka. Absolut even has its own museum, accessible

through the Web. The print campaign has won the kind of devotion from legions of young fans in a way that is usually reserved for television commercials. This is all the more remarkable because many of these fans aren't users of the product and weren't targets of the advertising. Wander around any college dorm and odds are fair you'll find more than a few rooms decorated with Absolut posters and ads.

When I mentioned the campaign to a thirty-one-year-old colleague, she came back the next day with a folder of hundreds of Absolut ads she had been tearing out of magazines since she was fourteen years old. She never drank Absolut then; she doesn't drink any liquor now. Although she managed to collect a great many of the six hundred-plus ads that have run in the last twenty or so years, she has contributed nothing to the 14,000 percent increase in sales that Absolut has recorded. (From fewer than twenty-thousand cases in 1979 when the campaign began, Absolut sold in excess of five million cases a year in the 1990s.)

This powerful fusion of art and advertising began when Michel Roux, then the president of Carillon Importers and a friend of Andy Warhol, asked Warhol to paint the Absolut bottle. Roux wasn't sure how he would use the painting. The Absolut campaign had been running for a while, but no artist had ever been commissioned.

That was 1985, and Absolut was a relative newcomer to the American market. When Absolut first came to the States in 1979, vodka was not a popular drink, and the most favored vodkas were always Russian. Absolut, created by Lars Olsson Smith in 1879, is made near Ahus, a small town in the south of Sweden. It uses a distillation process called rectification to gain added purity. The initial advertising focused on the "purity" of the drink. "Absolut Perfection" was the first headline, and the first bottle sported a glowing halo. From the outset the campaign followed a ruling convention of liquor

Absolut continues to identify with the arts. See **absolutearts.com** for an overview of the current art scene. They also have a devoted following of collectors. Try **absolut.intheunknown.net, home.swipnet.se, jennylynn.com,** and **absolutad.com** for lists of ads as well as articles written about the campaign.

advertising: make the bottle the hero. Getting Warhol to paint the hero, however, was anything but conventional and earned unconventional success. There is no better example of the symbiosis between high art and advertising.

As we've seen in an earlier chapter, pop artists took images from the land of mass media and objects from the world of mass production and gave their audience a new way of seeing them. Absolut gave such artists access to audiences larger than they had ever imagined. And it gave mass audiences a range of artistic styles and conceptions that they might not have otherwise had a chance to see. While the artists did great things for Absolut, it is also true that the campaign enhanced the careers of many an artist.

In the beginning, the reputations of Warhol, Keith Haring, whose ad ran after he died and gained even more notice as a result, and Ed Ruscha gave the campaign its cachet. Warhol's painting did more than turn the bottle into an icon; it made the bottle a subject for art. Now other artists could step up to the revered object and try their hand. In the world of Renaissance art, painters earned their reputations by taking on obligatory biblical scenes; similarly,

Roux enlisted a wide range of American artists to pay homage to his own halo-wearing heavenly spirit. And while the company was happy to use established artists, Roux made a point of looking for the unknown and surprising. FOR THE MOST PART, THE CAMPAIGN GAVE A LARGE AUDIENCE TO ARTISTS WHOM OTHERWISE HAD LITTLE HOPE OF FINDING ONE.

Interviewed in *Business Week,* for instance, Ron English recounted how "the Absolut thing completely changed my life. Before that, I had spent five years living in dire poverty on Avenue D in Manhattan. I couldn't even get galleries to look at slides of my work." After the ad ran, galleries wanted him, and Roux sent him on a tour of Japan, where he felt as if he were a celebrity.

Roux has his own version of class lust, but rather than using art to associate his product with the upper class, he uses it to appeal to people's sense of difference and daring. This is not class defined economically. It is identity marketing to anyone who wants to think of themselves as members of the class of people who are stylish, imaginative, avant-garde, hip, and wry. Not only did he make Absolut attractive by "discovering" new artists, Roux evoked those qualities in the ads.

He also ran his ads to reach communities where those qualities were valued, communities most advertisers found too controversial to court directly in the 1980s. Absolut lays claim to being the first mainstream advertiser to target the gay community in an ad that ran in *The Advocate.* Gay men appreciated the recognition. They asked for Absolut. The trend began. Just as Barratt, of Pears' soap fame, had targeted pregnant mothers, Roux understood that a little attention paid to an often-ignored class of people could yield significant rewards.

The best example of Roux's willingness to associate his product with the avant-garde is seen in an insert titled "Artists of the Nineties," which took artists whose reputations were considerably less than Warhol's and gave them real exposure. His interest in demographic power can be seen in two similar inserts he produced. One was filled with nothing but the work of African-American painters and another with only the work of gay and lesbian painters. This strategy was not just about the aesthetics, it was about the politics of art. By recognizing their existence, Roux asked these audiences to elect his product. If sales were any measure, he got their votes in a landslide.

Although they couldn't look more different, the real precursor to the Absolut campaign was the work for Container Corporation of America. Absolut was more interested in segmenting markets and selling cachet, but like CCA it recognized that cultural advocacy was a powerful tool. In fact, both campaigns commissioned a series of ads that celebrated the separate states of the United States and, in Absolut's case, great cities (New York, L.A., Paris, Berlin) where vodka flowed.

Like CCA, Absolut had a definite interest in the international scene. Probably the timeliest tactic in the whole range of Absolut advertising was the insert called "Absolut Glasnost" that ran, appropriately enough, in the magazine Andy Warhol founded, *Interview.*

Sending Paige Powell, *Interview's* ad director, to Russia, Michel Roux took advantage of a unique moment in the history of the twentieth century. The freedom of a democratic culture devoted to the pursuit of happiness and fueled by the fruits of capitalism's cornucopia turns art into a commodity. It is ironic that in totalitarian cultures, art matters more. The artists Powell recruited were painters who had spent their lives oppressed and hounded by the state. They painted for themselves and for each other. There was no market value for what they did. When their work showed up in *Interview,* that all changed. Some artists became more popular than others, some more critically acclaimed. Friends who had shown their work furtively to each other for support and criticism under the communist regime now became rivals as free market competition fueled the flames of difference.

Opposite: Keith Haring wanted to bring art to the public. He began by putting his icons on empty advertising billboards in the New York City subway.

The Absolut campaign was a perfect gallery.
Following Spread: Ed Ruscha, a friend of Warhol, did this early ad. From African-American artists (Adams) to Russians (Mitta and Kosolapov), Absolut used art to stay contemporary and to target niches.

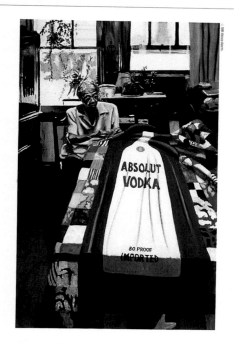

ABSOLUT ADAMS.

ABSOLUT MITTA.

ABSOLUT KOSOLAPOV.

As a result of the campaign, the Absolut bottle has become less an object in and of itself and more an opportunity for the purely subjective expression of personality, creativity, and individual vision. This idea that a bottle of spirits can be the inspiration for the artist, who in turn refashions reality so that we see it more acutely, with an angle of originality we on our own are not capable of, is at the core of Absolut's success. The booze inside—invisible, pure, fluid, without even the distinctiveness of taste—is the perfect tabula rasa. The various interpretations of its container have created a perceptual brew that enamors and intrigues watchers of every sort, from teenagers to their parents.

The success of the Absolut campaign as a stimulus to the imagination of a wide audience is inarguable. (Just check out any of the Web sites listed to get a vivid sense of how dedicated Absolut ad connoisseurs are.) Part of that success has to do with the particular moment in history when the campaign broke. Absolut, after all, had one unstated difference that made it particularly attractive in the U.S.A.: it wasn't made in the U.S.S.R. As good as Absolut on the rocks may be, it no doubt benefited from the fact that we were not in a cold war with Sweden. By continually reaching out to relatively unknown artists, Absolut stood up for the American ideal of freedom of expression that was so directly opposed to the collectivist ideas of all those vodka-producing manufacturers of the communist persuasion.

Using visually powerful, intellectually subtle images to brand its brand of vodka, Absolut created an arena of perception that not only defined itself but defined the way competitors would respond. Gorbachev's glasnost, while making it possible for Absolut to commission Russian artists to paint the Absolut bottle, also made it easier for Stolichnaya to compete against Absolut. Not coincidentally, the person who chose to take on Absolut on its own terms was none other than the man who had created the terms in the first place. When Absolut's distributer, Carillon, was absorbed by Seagram, Roux left Absolut. Moving on to the brand that had been his prime competitor, he attempted to do the same thing differently: he had Russian artists apply their skills to the Stoli bottle. But he took the strategy a step further.

Initially the campaign used the techniques of the posters of the October Revolution and over every ad stenciled the words "Freedom of Vodka." The phrase looked like the imprint of approval from a bureaucrat with a huge constructivist rubber stamp. Adopting Absolut's tactic of commissioning artists to "paint" the bottle, the ads focus was not on *purity* and imagination, but on *freedom* and imagination.

Here the bottle stands on a parapet with two massive statues of idealized workers. They are being rained upon by stars just like those on the American flag. The buildings in the background are a cityscape of factorylike structures. The two heroic worker-statues grasp bouquets of flowers in their hands, thrusting their arms in the air in the way they would if they were raising guns in a victory celebration.

The words "Freedom of Vodka" drip blue ink as if they had been slapped on in such a hurry that there was no time to do it right. They evoke political graffiti, painted in the blue blood of revolution, angrily defacing the scene. Following the lead of Absolut, the purveyors of Stoli have used art as a lens to focus on the new place of Russia in history.

This is not about the triumph of America over the Soviet Union, but about something even more essentially American— the rejection of and triumph over the past. Using art of the past to reject the past is one of the savvier ways to appropriate paintings to sell more mundane products. It affirms our deep-seated desire to ignore the burdens of history so that we can feel free to pursue whatever happiness the free market has to offer.

Opposite: Socialist Realism was art serving the propaganda needs of the Soviet state; advertising uses art as propaganda for capitalism's products. Stolichnaya played on the classic image of the triumphant worker, mixing one form of propaganda into another. To get a more complete view of the art of Socialist Realism, visit **marxists.org/subject/art/ visual_arts/painting/exhibits/ socialist-realism.**

STOLICHNAYA

Stolichnaya vodka

DISTILLED AND BOTTLED IN RUSSIA FOR VAO SOJUZPLODOIMPORT

FREEDOM OF VODKA

RUSSIAN VODKA

Whiskey Going to the Rackhouse to Age"—painted at the distillery by the famous artist, Thomas Hart Benton

88 years at fine whiskey-making

makes this whiskey good

IMPERIAL
Reg U.S Pat Off

Hiram Walker's Blended Whiskey

86 proof. The straight whiskies in this product are 4 years or more old. 30% straight whiskey. 70% grain neutral spirits. Hiram Walker & Sons Inc., Peoria, Ill.

It isn't surprising that this use of art as a type of identity marketing is best seen in two brands of liquor. After all, what product is more directly associated with escape, exhilaration, a relief from reality, and inspiration for the creative spirits among us than spirits themselves?

Neither Absolut nor Stoli discovered this association between spirits and the spirit of art. Courvoisier is one liquor producer who had previously used art in a more plodding and obvious way. Positioned as the brandy of Napoleon, Courvoisier ads set the bottle in front of heroic paintings of the renowned French general. Stoli used a style of art to align its product with the history of Russia so that it could position its product as having triumphed over that history. Courvoisier employs a less ambitious strategy. For Courvoisier, art functions as a highbrow form of testimonial argument. Portraits of the great man rest on desks or hang on walls with richly appointed interiors. Courvoisier's point couldn't get simpler: Napoleon chose this product; so should you.

Courvoisier followed their tactic wherever it took them. They used art to highlight the psychological power of Napoleon's personality in one instance, and, in another, they relied on art history per se. In this ad (upper left) we are told nothing about the product and everything about the painting, Karl von Steuben's *Retour de l'Île d'Elbe, Février 1815 (Return from the Isle of Elbe, February 1815)* where Napoleon challenges his troops to kill him and they instead embrace him, shouting "Long live the Emperor."

This story painting represents a French version of what in America might be described as "Miller time." But this isn't a moment when work is over and the guys can get together.

Courvoisier time is that moment when the Little General meets his destiny and is seen not just as Napoleon but as the soul of the French republic. Courvoisier is not just the brandy of Napoleon, it is the brandy of all Frenchmen. The ad is a good example of how art brings a wealth of associations to the service of a simple message—buy this bottle.

Courvoisier was itself using a technique that others had mined before. In the 1940s, Hiram Walker tried something similar to market Imperial whiskey. Hiram Walker used high art to ennoble the working man.

Portraying excellence as a function of working-class dedication is not a common position in advertising generally. Showing a factory is often too generic and less psychologically persuasive than associating your bottle with some clear aspiration (a rich home) or wish fulfillment (a beautiful girl) or the warmth of a community of friends. Existing paintings that made heroes of working men were few and not particularly famous. Hiram Walker didn't inhabit a world where the company could consider having artists paint its bottle as an object of imaginative playfulness and reverie. There was no reason to associate its brand with the chic world of art. In the

Opposite: In 1934, Thomas Hart Benton became the first artist ever featured on the cover of *Time* magazine. For an interesting sense of his work, go to

catherton.com and click on Benton for quick access to the paintings and sketches he did to chronicle life in the U.S. Navy.

1940s that world was more bohemian and less accessible than it was in the 1980s.

A different version of this strategy did, however, make sense in the context of a country that was returning home from war. Coming at the end of World War II, Hiram Walker commissioned Thomas Hart Benton to go to its distillery and create a portrait of its factory. Having entered the war late, America provided the difference between victory and defeat by converting the nation into a huge armaments factory. The war, Winston Churchill had noted, was won with British courage, Russian blood, and American industry. So immortalizing your factory was not, in 1946, quite as offbeat an idea as it might seem today.

This ad (see page 120), the caption tells us, was "painted at the distillery by the famous artist Thomas Hart Benton" (in case you weren't sure why Hiram Walker had chosen him). Titled "Whiskey on its way to Age," it portrays workers rolling barrels in the cellar of a distillery. The only other writing is a headline, typographically modest, affirming that Imperial whiskey has been around for eighty-eight years and is committed to aging the product to make it "good."

After sixty years of advertising hyperbole, a claim such as "good" may sound strangely modest. But it fits the tone and style of the painting perfectly. It is how the men in the painting would speak, and reflects the abiding homespun spirit of the place the painting evokes.

Courvoisier may be the brandy of Napleon, Absolut the vodka of Warhol and the cognoscenti, and Stoli the spirit of freedom-loving Russians, but Hiram Walker, the art of its advertising tells us, is the whiskey of American workers.

Not surprisingly, you can't leave this category without coming around to face Michel Roux once more. This time he's looking for his own personal hat trick. What he did for Absolut, and again for Stolichnaya (sales went from 950,000 cases to about 1.15 million in a couple of years), he is now trying to do for Absente. This time he is following the age-old dictum: the good borrow, the great steal. In this case he has the privilege of stealing from himself.

Where Absolut was the icon painted by pop, and Stoli a pop version of socialist realism, Absente is the drink of high culture, pure and simple. Its first fans were Van Gogh, Toulouse-Lautrec, Paul Verlaine, Ernest Hemingway, and Oscar Wilde, the Web site tells us. We are given appropriate quotations, such as this gem from Wilde: "After the first glass, you see things as you wish they were. After the second, you see things as they are not. Finally, you see things as they really are, and this is the most horrible thing in the world." What's more, you can buy any of the Absente posters. They are done, as Absolut once was, by artists known only to those who follow the always-changing world of galleries and avant-garde presentations—Ron English, John Pacovsky, Alain Despert, Giancarlo Impiglia, and Alex Echo among others.

The jury is out on Roux's latest gambit. BUT AS A STRATEGY, IT CONFIRMS THAT THE LAND WHERE ART AND COMMERCE MEET CONTINUES TO BE A FERTILE PLACE FOR MARKETERS WHO ARE WILLING TO TAKE RISKS AND COURT CONTROVERSY.

Opposite: Absente.com gets you all the art and posters of the current campaign. **Modbooks.com/ absinthe** gives you a concise history of the drink.

Hbd.org/brewery/library/ absfaq.html gives you the science of absinthe.

ABSINTHE REFINED

By Ron English

Entropy reigns and advertising overwhelms us all. Kitsch rules. Art adjusts by prompting outrage and making ads. Imitation, appropriation, and conceptual art become the new brushes that paint a pretty picture. Or, I've been art so long it looks like advertising to me.

THE GREATEST DE-GEN-ERATION

"Bad taste is real taste, of course, and good taste is the residue of someone else's privilege."
DAVE HICKEY

"It used to be that people needed products to survive. Now products need people to survive."
NICHOLAS JOHNSON

"Today's smartest advertising style is tomorrow's corn."
WILLIAM BERNBACH

ARTISTS ARE MORE THAN WILLING to hire themselves out to corporations to sell products.

IS THIS A FURTHER DEGENERATION INTO KITSCH, OR A REGENERATION OF POLITICAL AND SOCIAL AWARENESS?

In the last thirty years or so, whatever tension existed between the creators of art and the makers of advertising has been diminished by a culture industry driven to obliterate all boundaries. Critics are left to draw the latest line in the sand, only to watch it be washed away by the next new wave.

The process started with Dada and Duchamp, then found its most public voice with pop and Warhol in the early 1960s. Since then, artists have launched all kinds of forays into the wilds of advertising, a movement matched only by advertising's sorties into the art world. While obvious distinctions still exist, the endeavors' differences are now more blurred than ever. What were once censured practices rarely raise an eyebrow anymore. Artists are more than willing to hire themselves out to corporations to sell products, with little fear of damaging their reputations. Hiring artists is no longer a strategy limited to high-minded corporate campaigns, such as the Container Corporation of America's, or to provocative breakthroughs, such as Absolut's. It is open to anyone who has anything to sell, from beer to inkjet printers. More important, artists cross the line into the commercial world without looking back. To work for a branded patron does not necessarily devalue your brand of art.

At the beginning of the twentieth century, art that took as its subject the nature of art defined the avant-garde. By the end of the century, the cutting edge was defined by art that took as its subject the nature of advertising. Artists are no longer content to use the content of advertising as the subject of their work. They now feel free to appropriate the *forms* and *attitudes* of advertising to express their point of view. Still, working in this area certainly opened artists up to a distinct kind of criticism. Indeed, most any artist who used advertising as a form was likely to be called out in terms usually reserved for advertisers: self-promoting salesmen, glib mass-producers, and self-serving purveyors of the art of branding themselves.

This blurring of boundaries, the overlapping of high and low culture, was notable decades ago, as the much-discussed *High and Low: Modern Art and Popular Culture* show at the Museum of Modern Art in 1990 made clear. The exhibition riled defenders of high culture, beauty, taste, and standards, if only because it illustrated how common it was for advertising and art to feed on each other. This symbiotic relationship between art and its alter ego—kitsch—has attracted a lot of critical attention over the years. The first and best declaration of this critique was Clement Greenberg's 1939 *Partisan Review* essay, "Avant-Garde and Kitsch."

Greenberg was not happy. Kitsch, he argued, was on its way to overwhelming all indigenous cultures and was "becoming a universal culture, the first universal culture ever beheld." Greenberg defined kitsch as "popular, commercial art and literature with their chromeotypes, magazine covers, illustrations, ads, slick and pulp fiction, comics, Tin Pan Alley music, tap dancing, Hollywood movies, etc., etc." Kitsch had grown out of the needs of a new class of people. As the Industrial Revolution attracted people to cities, the entertainments rural life had provided were left behind, in part because workers had to become literate. When people weren't working, they discovered leisure time and its dark shadow, boredom. "To fill the demand of the new market a new commodity was devised: ersatz culture, kitsch, destined for those who, insensible to the values of genuine culture, are hungry nevertheless for the diversion that only culture of some sort can provide." With the advent of mass production, culture for profit takes over from folk culture. Once these items of culture were sold in large numbers, America became immersed in kitsch, in all its egalitarian, democratic, commercial, and vulgar energy.

Kitsch and the Internet were made for each other. To shop for kitsch try **kitsch.co.uk** or **worldofkitsch.com**. To explore movie-related kitsch there's **dollsoup.co.uk**. For famous kitsch art go to **keane-eyes.com,** and to experience the most successful art of the kitsch culture, go to **thomaskinkade.com.** For a fuller view of kitsch culture, go to **museumofbadart.com**. For books, essays and links go to **diabooks.org** as well as **eserver.org.**

KITSCH usurped high art's role in defining the culture to itself. Not coincidentally, this era also saw the beginnings of the modern advertising industry. In fact, the remarkable rise of advertising has provoked many a pundit to announce its centrality in the development of Greenberg's "universal culture."

At the beginning of the pop movement, when Richard Hamilton was formulating a definition of pop that was synonymous with the attitudes and qualities of advertising, his colleagues in the Independent Group at the Institute of Contemporary Arts in London, Alison and Peter Smithson, wrote that "advertising has caused a revolution in the popular art field. Advertising has become respectable in its own right and is beating the fine arts at their old game. . . . And the transient thing is making a bigger contribution to our visual climate than any of the traditional fine arts."

That was in 1956, before the proliferation of magazine culture, before every household had a television set, before every television set was color, before satellite TV brought us five hundred channels. The mass of mass culture has snowballed since then. Andy Warhol's most astute realization, according to Marc Aronson, was that "in an age that glorified television, advertisement, and market research, the avant-garde did not have to be against mass culture. Mass culture already was avant-garde." But pop itself was soon overwhelmed by the rush of mass culture. There was simply too much of everything. Pop artists, like the citizen-consumers they painted for, found themselves swimming in a visual sea, pounded by a surfeit of images, products, and selling arguments. It may have once been radical to paint the mundane, but one day the radical ceased being new and a painting of the mundane became just another mundane painting.

The next step was not merely to put the images of advertising on to a canvas with pop élan and acceptance, but to use the methods of advertising to expose the underlying ideology

Above: The covers for pulp fiction paperbacks turned every drugstore and bookstore into a gallery for kitsch art.

AMERICAN CYANAMID

AMERICAN CYANAMID is the parent of BRECK® Inc., maker of the shampoo which keeps the Breck Girl's hair clean, shining and beautiful.

AMERICAN CYANAMID does more for women. It knows: "We really don't run a health spa."

And therefore those of its female employees of child-bearing age who are exposed to toxic substances are now given a choice.

They can be reassigned to a possibly lower paying job within the company. They can leave if there is no opening. Or they can have themselves sterilized and stay in their old job.

Four West Virginia women chose sterilization.
AMERICAN CYANAMID...

Where Women have a Choice

of capitalism. This new generation of artists appropriated advertising to criticize the culture that spawned it. This was not a further degeneration into kitsch, as Greenberg would have it. It was, rather, a regeneration of political and social awareness. Beginning in the 1970s and continuing into the next century, this response to the pervasiveness of American consumerism was hardly confined to America's shores; the artists who explored it were as readily found in London as they were in New York.

Provoked and inspired by the frenzy of advertising surrounding them in the '80s and '90s, this post-pop generation took art in a new direction. For these artists, the art is the ad and the ad is the art. Each one wants you to confront the complex relationship between the two mediums and the commercial culture that spawns them. In the work of Hans Haacke, Barbara Kruger, Jenny Holzer, Richard Prince, Damien Hirst, and Jeff Koons, among others, we are face to face with a measure of just how useful a form advertising has become in the world of art.

The boundaries between art, advertising, and journalism are inextricably entwined in Hans Haacke's work. Like journalism, the goal of Haacke's art is to afflict the comfortable and to comfort the afflicted. To tell *his* truth, he doesn't paint, or write an essay; he chooses the form best known for telling half-truths. Ironic and polemical, this kind of appropriation is a long way from Warhol's reproductions of commercial images. Warhol uses commercial images to celebrate their cultural complexity, he paints their surfaces but he doesn't alter their message. He wants us to enjoy the world created by the wizards of business and celebrity he envies and admires. Haacke, on the other hand, demands that we pay attention to the corporate wizards behind the curtain of media so he can expose their venal motives and antisocial effects. Much of his work uses the templates of advertising to undercut corporate authority and expose the fatuousness of

advertising's arguments. Attacking the work-place safety of American Cyanamid in *The Right to Life,* for example, Haacke appropriates the Breck girl's image and uses the language of consumer-product selling to expose the antisocial behavior of the seller. This work never runs in magazines, but it gets the attention of advertisers nonetheless. In the early '80s, when Haacke did a series of works which appropriated Mobil Oil's editorial ads, Mobil lawyers managed to stop the Tate from publishing a catalogue of the work for a full year.

Turning the powerfully persuasive methods of advertising on the motives of the advertisers is only one way these artists of the borderland between commerce and art are holding a mirror up to the murky cultural divide. Barbara Kruger, for instance, uses the visual grammar of advertising to pursue a cultural critique from a feminist perspective. Starting at *Mademoiselle* magazine, she became their head designer at the age of 22. Her background in commerce led her to belie the distinction between that world and the supposedly more meaningful world of galleries and museums. Her 1981 show, *Pictures and Promises: A Display of Advertising, Slogans, and Interventions*, brought advertisements themselves onto the gallery wall to do for them, in a sense, what Duchamp had done for the urinal.

Her subsequent work—assertive, demanding, provocative, political, and subversive—looks and acts pretty much like advertising does. It doesn't present her point of view; it sells it. Kruger, like Haacke, wants to provoke a political awareness in the viewer. In addition, her critics will be quick to tell you, she wants to promote Barbara Kruger as a brand. She does T-shirts and bags and soap and scarves as well, and in her show in the late '80s she had a room filled with products that carried her ad-like headlines. More importantly, she puts her artwork in all the places you expect to see advertising: on billboards, bus shelters, and the walls of abandoned buildings. By treating New York City as if it were

Opposite: The appropriation of advertising to criticize advertisers is one response to the rise of American consumerism and the success of global capitalism.

Following Spread: Barbara Kruger's art appropriates the visual grammar of advertising to make a political point. Rostov vodka appropriates her art to create a brand image.

Your body is a battleground

It was the
worst of times
It was the
worst of times

Free yourself from the misery of a futile **existence**

a gallery, she illustrates how art has adopted the more assertive and public posture of advertising. Like Jenny Holzer and Keith Haring, she would rather bring her art to the customers than wait for the customers to come to her. It comes as no surprise to see advertisers turn the tables using Kruger's brand image to purvey their own products. Rostov vodka uses her black-and-red poster form; it echoes the Russian constructivists and thereby gives an appropriate nod to Kruger's own anticapitalist message. The effect is to generate a powerful, distinctly angry, and politically witty campaign to make people aware of yet another Russian vodka.

Jenny Holzer also has taken the basic advertising form of the headline and made it all her own. Her *Truisms* project garnished New York walls, marquees, kiosks, and construction fences. When asked why she used text as a medium, she said she expressed her art in words "because I couldn't figure out how to paint what I meant." Her axioms read just like headlines.

ANY SURPLUS IS IMMORAL
KEEP SOMETHING IN RESERVE FOR
    EMERGENCIES
MONEY CREATES TASTE
MORALS ARE FOR LITTLE PEOPLE
REDISTRIBUTING WEALTH IS IMPERATIVE

In using an art of words to make us think twice about the bromides and received opinions we don't usually take time to think about, Holzer gives us art that could easily be mistaken for advertising. Compare, for instance, a sampling of the current campaign for Citibank. As with Holzer's *Truisms*, the campaign is all words, and runs where people live. It is on the sides of buses and on billboards. What's more, its theme, "Live richly," is persuasively ironic; one of the world's largest banks is trying to win your business by telling you how important it is to believe that money, as Holzer might have written, can't buy happiness. Or, as the bank's all-type billboards say:

NEVER CONFUSE YOUR MEANS
    WITH YOUR MEANING.
MAY ALL YOUR JOYS BE PUBLICLY
    TRADED.
DEFER TAXES, NOT RETIREMENT.
NEVER MIND THE COST OF LIVING,
    HAVE YOU SEEN THE COST OF
    LEARNING?

Another type of appropriation follows the path of Dada and pop more directly. These artists are not so aggressively polemical. They take advertisements at their face value and use them to propose their own conception of the relationships between art, advertising, the commercialized world, and their own political points of view.

Richard Prince received a good deal of attention in the early '80s by becoming the most straightforward of those artists who show you what to look at, but don't necessarily create the thing you're looking at. Duchamp created this approach in 1913 when he mounted a bicycle wheel on a stool in a gallery. Calling such found objects "readymades"—his gallery-mounted urinal, *The Fountain*, remains the most famous example— his was the first in a long line of such gestures, from Jasper Johns's bronzed Ballantine ale cans to Jeff Koons's suspended Hoover vacuum cleaners. Prince simply took the iconic cowboy image from the Marlboro ads, photographed it, enlarged it and hung it in a gallery. The point, as effective as it was obvious, generated a host of mixed feelings about the promise of American indi-

Right: Jenny Holzer's axioms go everywhere. Placing them on customized LED screens succeeds in getting you to think as much about the medium as the message.

Opposite: The indelible power of advertising imagery is made clear in Richard Prince's famous series. Can you see the cowboy without seeing his brand of cigarette?

JEFF KOONS

Dd Ee Ff Gg Hh Ii Jj Kk Ll Mm Nn Oo

EXPLOIT THE MASSES

MENTALITY

BANALITY AS SAVIOUR

SONNABEND • NEW YORK   MAX HETZLER • KÖLN   DONALD YOUNG • CHICAGO

vidualism and the complex ways that promise is used to inspire people to buy things that may not serve them well.

Jeff Koons has become the most well known of the artists who work in the borderland where art and advertising converge. In a 1986 interview with Klaus Ottman, Koons made his view of advertising's role in the culture clear. "It's basically the medium that defines people's perceptions of the world, of life itself, how to interact with others."

When Koons takes the ads for Frangelico liqueur (the irony that this product is named for a great Renaissance painter cannot have been lost on him) and Gordon's gin and has them silk-screened and then puts them on the wall of a gallery, his intention is both political and aesthetic."... These liquor ads... were targeted to drinking audiences at different income levels... It's very clear... that the more money you make, the more abstraction that's laid on you. In this series I was telling people not to give up their economic power—that this pursuit of luxury was a form of degradation and not to get debased by it." Koons's comment reveals his sense of himself as the artist-hero of consumer consciousness. "I believe that my art gets across the point that I'm in this morality theater trying to help the underdog." It's just this kind of talk that gets critics hopping. As Robert Hughes put it, "If Jeff Koons's work is about class struggle, I am Maria of Romania."

Whatever critics may say, Koons is not shy about telling his audience what his work means or reticent about promoting it in ways that most artists shy away from. He went so far as to create advertisements for himself as art—big, glossy numbers tuned to his target market of *Artforum* and *Art in America* readers—to build the audience for his gallery shows. (He was also, he says, making a point about banality.) Such brash self-promotion has made him a lightning rod for critics who decry the increasing collusion between art and the kitsch culture of advertising and consumerism. But for all that, Koons and a host of others move freely in both worlds.

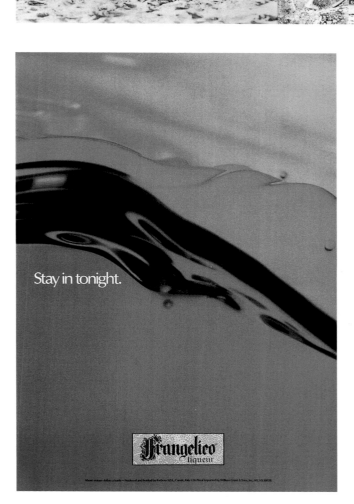

Opposite and Above: Jeff Koons's tactics of advertising himself and remaking unaltered ads to explore the values of banality make it impossible to discern the distinction between art and advertising.

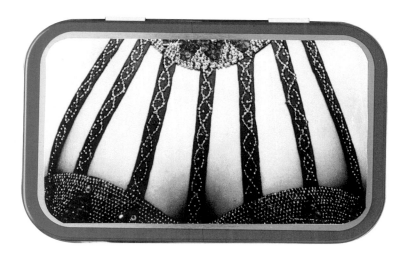

Beck's beer, for instance, hired Damien Hirst to adapt one of his spot paintings for a label as part of their market plan to target trendsetters. What Absolut did for vodka, Beck's would do for beer. Of course the Hirst bottles commanded a premium price to boot. Beck's has gone even further in aligning itself with art. The company runs a competition for young artists in which the winner gets to design a label for the bottle. It's the biggest monetary art prize in Britain, paying over thirty thousand dollars. Reflecting on the easy commerce between art and commodity products, other conceptual artists have even created work that comments on the willingness of their colleagues to sell their skills to advertisers.

Tracey Emin, the well-known, outrage-courting young British contemporary of Hirst, actually opened an "art-junk" store in 1993 as a work of art. (It made money.) Working with another artist, Sarah Lucas, she created and sold ashtrays with Damien Hirst's face on the bottom. Hirst had become famous for, among other things, suspending cows and sheep and shark in formaldehyde; the mystery of mortality was his subject. Giving consumers the chance to put their cigarettes out on his image is as artful as ashtrays get. Emin, both commentator and participant, is happy to throw her own brand into the commercializing fray as well. She has sold the use of her face to the people who want you to drink Bombay Blue Sapphire gin. Since the eyes are the windows to the soul, having her eyes colored the sky blue of the bottle is no doubt telling us something about the spirit of art.

Like Beck's beer, Altoids is a brand heavily invested in associating itself with the art world. The "curiously strong" candy has begun what it calls its "Curiously Strong Collection;" a patron of younger artists, the company purchases each year thirty works of art priced under twenty-five hundred dollars. In addition, it hires young artists like Jessica Craig-Martin to do illustrations for their tin box.

Above: Even packaging is now a province for artists. Damien Hirst's fresh-as-springtime design for Camel cigarettes gives smokers an image that's both attractive and ironic. Given the opportunity to use the Altoid's tin as her canvas, Jessica Craig-Martin gave it a curiously sexy image to go with the curiously strong taste.

The list of crossovers is long and prestigious. Nan Goldin, like Damien Hirst, designed packs for Camel cigarettes and did brochures for Matsuda, the clothing designer. "They put out a little book called *Naked in New York* and I got more attention for that than I got for twenty years of my work," she recalled in a recent interview. Even industrial manufacturers such as Xerox have hired artists to help them sell their products.

Creating art in a tradition that runs from Duchamp to Warhol to Prince to Koons, artists who work in what Walter Benjamin labeled the "age of mechanical reproduction" have persistently wrestled with the relationship between the original and the copy. So it seems apt that the company synonymous with copying has gotten into the art game. Xerox invented the technology that revolutionized office work by giving ordinary people the power to duplicate their words and images and spread them around. By democratizing the power to create copies that looked exactly like their originals, Xerox became the fastest growing corporation in the history of America until the advent of Microsoft. When the company decided to enter the consumer market for color ink-jet printers, it turned to art to get itself noticed.

George Rodrigue, a regional American painter, had created a popular icon known as Blue Dog. His paintings were in the pop tradition and had garnered a large following; capitalizing on the popularity of Blue Dog, Xerox commissioned Rodrigue to create paintings for their color inkjet printers (see page 139). Warhol had taken objects from a retail shelf and put them on the gallery wall. Rodrigue's Blue Dog, having earned its fame in the gallery, was now enlisted to sell products off a retail shelf. Rodrigue decided to close the loop by making original paintings of the ads that had used his original paintings to sell color inkjets that could print copies of his originals. Following the pop tactic of magnifying commercial imagery, these magazine-sized ads became canvases five

TASTE. AND SEE

BOMBAY SAPPHIRE

Uniquely distilled with 10 botanicals.

Tracey Emin, Artist, photographed by Malcolm Venville

feet high and three feet wide. They had the headlines, the product, the body copy of the original ads. Rodrigue could sell the use of his images to an advertiser, but he could also bring them back into the gallery. In the end, he wanted both customers and connoisseurs to know who was in control.

An even more conceptual example of this crossover also involves Xerox. In this case the company hired one of the most provocative of the so-called Young British Artists made

Above: Tracey Emin's work is often outrageously personal. Her most famous piece, *Everyone I Have Ever Slept With (1963-1995)*, is a tent with names sewn, quilt-like, on the inside. The Bombay ad, headlined "Taste and See," is not only a testimonial for the good taste of the gin, but is also a challenge any artist might make to her public. Emin is, after all, famous for ignoring the boundaries of good taste by exploiting all aspects of her private life.

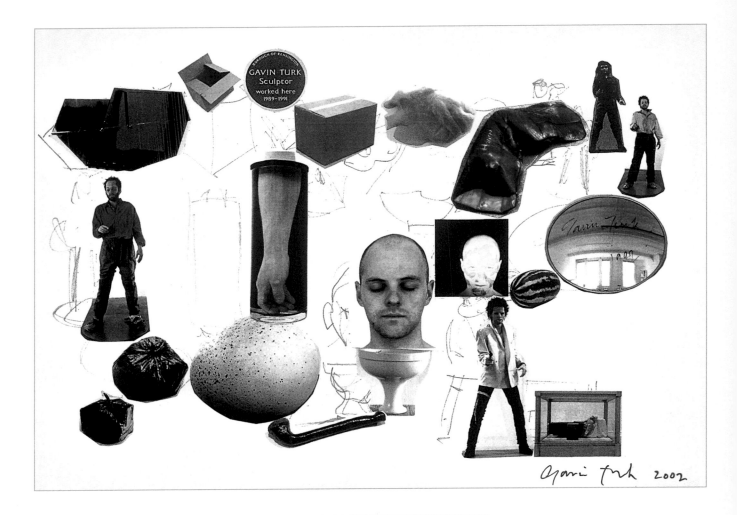

Gavin Turk 2002

"For the first time ever, images of art have become ephemeral, ubiquitous, insubstantial, available, valueless, free."

JOHN BERGER

10p

Another Young British Artist sells a piece of their work for a ridiculous amount of money.

How much could you pay for a signed piece of work by a famous Young British Artist: £5,000, £10,000 or a whole lot more?

But, how much *should* you pay? And *who* sets the price anyway?

Well, on Wednesday 18th September, Gavin Turk will be turning the 'value of art' on its head. Using affordable digital technology – the new

Xerox DocuColor 2240 – he'll be creating perfect colour copies of his work, signing them and then selling them for the price it costs to print them. Just 10p!

This will be happening in the Clore Foyer, at Tate Britain, for 45 minutes only from 12.30pm.

So come along and buy one. Who knows how much your 10p print will be worth in the future?

There's a new way to look at things.

THE DOCUMENT COMPANY
XEROX.

©2002 XEROX CORPORATION. All rights reserved. XEROX, The Document Company® and There's a new way to look at things® are trademarks of XEROX CORPORATION.

famous in *Sensation*, the exhibition of work from the stash of adman cum art collector Charles Saatchi. The only ad involved in this promotion touted the fact that Gavin Turk was going to create an original work, sign it, and sell copies of the signed original for only ten pence, the cost of making a color print. Taking on the project, Turk created a montage made up of copies of his most famous work, a visual résumé of a career wholly devoted to exploring the relationship between originals and copies, between authenticity and imitation. The Xerox printer/copier was set up in the garden of Tate

Britain, next to a Gavin Turk sculpture that rests on the lawn in front of the building, and Turk made copies and signed them. Hundreds of people stood in line for an hour to buy one each for ten pence; no doubt some anticipated selling their copies on eBay for considerably more. In this work the consumer/collector became a dealer/entrepreneur, and the artist of originals became the producer of copies whose value resided not simply in the object but in the signature. This moment, like Turk's work in general, stimulates us to think about how creations reflect and reproduce themselves. What's the original? What's the copy? What's art? What's advertising?

These questions have also preoccupied Michael Galbreth and Jack Massing as well. They call themselves the Art Guys and have made a career as conceptual artists who satirize the morals and mores of commercialism. Their most notable work in this vein was *Suits: The Clothes Make the Man*. They wore grey-flannel Todd Oldham suits plastered with the logos of Target, Timex, Absolut, and the like. The companies paid for the space; as per the advertising contract, the artists wore the suits to every public appearance for a year. The avant-garde becomes the rear-garde; the artist becomes the advertiser while using pointedly self-effacing humor to mount a lighthearted critique of the culture of selling.

Unlike the passionately ideological critique of artists like Haacke, Holzer, and Kruger, the Art Guys's tactic is to co-opt the power of advertising by deflating it. Dick Detzner, a Chicago-based contemporary, takes that anti-corporate satire and renders it in a more painterly way. Mixing Renaissance images, advertising icons, a painter's brushwork, and the visual rhetoric of political cartooning, he created a body of work he called *Corporate Sacrilege*. His rendition of the *Last Supper*, populated by the critters and characters who represent some of America's most famous brands, is yet another example of high and low mingling to generate a hybrid work typical of the art created in the borderland where kitsch and high culture collide.

All this work suggests how hard it is to mark the lines between high art and low culture. We live in a borderland where art and advertising are joined and reflect on each other in all the ways imaginations can conjure. Advertising not only hires artists, it has evolved into something of an art form

---

Opposite: Selling a visual résumé of the work that made Gavin Turk famous for "a ridiculous amount of money" is both a comment on the values of art and the low cost of reproduction. **Above (left):** Rodrigue did Blue Dog paintings for specific Xerox ads. **(right)** He then used those ads as subjects for new paintings. The journey from work of art to retail sales and back to the gallery wall increased the audience for his work. **Georgerodrigue.com** shows more.

[138 | 139]
Chapter 9 / THE GREATEST
DEGENERATION

itself. It no longer is a medium that only tells people what products do; it creates images that tell people what things mean. And that world of consumer desires it expresses provides a new range of subjects for contemporary artists to plumb. "I am interested," conceptual artist Sherrie Levine says, "in that area where the commodity meets the sublime." One can look at the art of these borderland artists and see it as the degeneration of a once great high culture or as the regeneration of a still dynamic and living one. Dave Hickey, the iconoclastic art critic, cogently observes that we live in a mercantile democracy where there are essentially two symbiotic modes of art. We have "commercial popular art that informs the culture," and "non-commercial academic art that critiques it," and we should never forget that "even though most popular art exploits the vernacular, some popular art redeems it—even though it's still for sale."

The real materials borderland artists work with are not ads, icons, or ideologies. What they turn into art is the roiling paradox of democratic capitalism. They see the same world we do. Commercial culture entertains and enlightens while it plays to the lowest common denominator. Mass production commodifies and cheapens everything while it generates prosperity and makes more things affordable for more people. Corporations heady with global ambitions manipulate and profiteer while they employ and produce. Pledging allegiance to the pursuit of happiness creates a land of selfish narcissists while it continues to motivate communities of hard-working immigrants.

Selling, in this borderland of paradox, is not all bad, despite what the dictionary says. In the balance between kitsch and art, between advertising and high culture, between exploitation and self-expression, the most reasonable response may be to revel in the constant stream of images, ads, art, and ideas, to keep an open mind, and make the most of it. Artist and citizen, advertiser and consumer, it's the American way of keeping life new.

Above: Dick Detzner's intent is to satirize the reverence people have for the sweet-natured icons of advertising who tell us the stories about their products. By altering high-art religious paintings with the lesser deities of Madison Avenue, he crossed boundaries that stimulated outrage and praise. Try **detzner.com** to see the whole series.

Opposite: The Art Guys didn't sell their souls, just every inch of ad space on their suits.

NOTES

Numbers preceding entries refer to page numbers.

4: Henry Ford, *Chicago Tribune*, May 25, 1916.

7: Andrew Zipern, *New York Times*, December, 20, 2001.

8: *Webster's New Collegiate Dictionary* (Springfield, Mass: G & C Merriam Company, 1979).

8: Hilton Kramer, in Steven Henry Madoff, ed., *Pop Art: A Critical History* (Berkeley: University of California Press, 1997), p. 69.

9: Claes Oldenburg, exhibition catalogue, *Environments, Situations, Spaces*, Martha Jackson Gallery, May-June 1961. Reprinted in Madoff, p. 213.

13: William Allen White, quoted in John P. Bradley, et. al., *The International Dictionary of Thoughts* (Chicago: J. G. Ferguson Publishing Co. 1969), p. 15.

13: John Kenneth Galbraith, quoted in Michael Jackman, *Book of Political Quotations* (New York: Crown Publishing Inc., 1982), p. 1.

15: Mark Twain, *A Connecticut Yankee in King Arthur's Court* (New York: Bantam Books, 2001).

27: John Berger, *Ways of Seeing* (London: British Broadcasting Corp., 1977), p. 33.

27: J. B. Priestley, quoted in Edward F. Murphy, *The Crown Treasury of Relevant Quotations* (New York: Crown Publishers, 1978), p. 14.

27: Jerry Della Femina, *From Those Wonderful Folks Who Gave You Pearl Harbor* (New York: Pocket Book, 1971), p. 256.

39: Berger, Ibid., p. 54.

39: John Lahr, quoted in Robert Andrews, *The Columbia Dictionary of Quotations* (New York: Columbia University Press, 1993), p. 19.

39: David Ogilvy, *Confessions of an Advertising Man* (New York: Atheneum, 1988), p. 118.

40: G. K. Chesterton, *Illustrated London News*, May 5, 1928.

43: Leo Burnett, *100 Leo's* (Chicago: Leo Burnett Company, 1955), p. 18.

44: Marlene Dietich, quotationspage.com

54: Mark Twain, "Down the Rhone," *Europe and Elsewhere* (New York: Harper & Brothers, 1923).

54: E. H. Gombrich, *The Story of Art* (New York: Phaidon, 1954), p. 218.

54: Edgar Quinet, *The Italian Revolution*, in *Complete Works*, Vol. 2 (Paris: Hachette, 1904), p. 133.

56: Donald Sassoon, *Becoming Mona Lisa: The Making of A Global Icon* (New York: Harcourt, Inc., 2001).

66: Oscar Wilde, "The Critic as Artist," in *The Works of Oscar Wilde* (London and Glasgow: Collins, 1948), p. 968.

69: Ekow Eshun, review of *Surrealism: Desire Unbound*, Tate@BBC, Nov. 16, 2002, p. 3.

69: Leo Steinberg, "Contemporary Art and the Plight of Its Public," quoted in Gregory Battock, *The New Art* (New York: E. P. Dutton and Company, Inc., 1966), p. 31.

75: Salvador Dali, quoted in Jennifer Mundy, ed., *Surrealism: Desire Unbound* (London: Tate Publishing, 2001), p. 37.

83: Alan Magee, "Works and Day," *Graphis*, No. 332 (2001).

83: Bruce Barton, in James B. Simpson, *Contemporary Quotations* (Binghampton, N.Y.: Vail-Ballou Press, 1964), p. 82.

83: Norman Douglas, quoted in Robert Andrews, *The Routledge Dictionary of Quotations* (London: Routledge & Kegan Paul, 1987), p. 5.

84: Walter Paepke, "Art In Industry," in Paul Theobald, *Modern Art in Advertising* (Chicago: Container Corporation of America, 1946), p. 2.

86: Ibid.

86: Michelle Bogart, *Artists, Advertising and The Borders of Art* (Chicago: University of Chicago Press, 1995).

86: Daniel Catton Rich, in Theobald, p. 1.

87: Herbert Bayer in John Massey, ed., *The Great Ideas of Western Man* (Chicago: University of Chicago Press, 1995), p. xi.

90: Walter Gropius, see architeturamoderna.com

90: Obituary for Gyorgy Kepes, MIT Newsletter, March 2002.

91: David Ogilvy, quoted in Massey, p. x.

97: Jed Perl, *Gallery Going* (New York: Harcourt Brace, 1995), p. 272.

97: Tilman Osterworld, *Pop Art* (Cologne, Germany: Taschen, 1999), p. 9.

97: Richard Hamilton, *Collected Words* (London: Thames and Hudson, 1982), p. 78.

98: Hamilton, p. 28.

98: David McCarthy, *Pop Art* (London: Tate Gallery Publishing, 2000).

99: Tom Wolfe, *The Painted Word* (New York: Farrar, Straus and Giroux, 1975).

101: McCarthy, p. 19.

101: Victor Bockris, *The Life and Death of Andy Warhol* (New York: Bantam Books, 1989), p. 110.

103: Roy Lichtenstein, quoted in Madoff, p. 370.

104: Lawrence Alloway, "Popular Culture and Pop Art," *Studies in Popular Communication*, Panthe Record 7, 1969, p. 52.

104: Hilton Kramer, in Madoff, p. 69.

104: Max Kozloff, "Art International," March 1962, reprinted in Madoff, p. 32.

104: Jules Langsner, "Art International," September 1962, reprinted in Madoff, Ibid., p. 33.

104: Andy Warhol and Pat Hackett, *POPism: The Warhol Sixties* (New York: Harcourt, Brace, Jovanovich, 1980), p. 39.

106: Andy Warhol, quoted in Robert Hughes, "The New York Review of Books," February 18, 1962, p. 8, reprinted in Madoff, p. 379.

106: Andy Warhol, *Andy Warhol, The Philosophy of Andy Warhol (From A to B and Back Again)* (New York: Harcourt, Brace and Company, 1975), p. 96.

106: Warhol, p. 144.

106: Warhol, p. 148, passim.

107: Warhol, pp. 100-101.

107: Peter Selz, "The Flaccid Art," *Partisan Review*, Summer 1963, pp. 313-16, reprinted in Madoff, p. 86.

109: Raymond Williams, *Problems in Materialism and Culture* (London: Verso, 1980), p. 184.

111: Warhol, p.92.

111: Leo Burnett, *100 Leo's* (Chicago: Leo Burnett Company, 1955), p. 8.

111: Marshall McLuhan, "Advertising Age," Sept. 3, 1976.

125: Dave Hickey, *Air Guitar, Essays on Art and Democracy* (Los Angeles: Art Issues Press, 1997), p. 54.

125: Nicholas Johnson, quoted in Jackman, p. 2.

125: William Bernbach, quoted in *Bill Bernbach Said . . .* (New York: DDB Needham Worldwide, 1989).

126: Clement Greenberg, "Avant-Garde and Kitsch," in *Partisan Review*, Fall 1939, pp. 34-49, passim.

127: Peter and Allison Smithson, *Ark*, November 1956, reprinted in Madoff, p. 4.

127: Mark Aronson, *Art Attack: A Short Cultural History of The Avant-Garde* (New York: Clarion Books, 1998), p. 141.

135: Jeff Koons, interview by Klaus Ottman, *Journal of Contemporary Art*, 1988.

135: Jeff Koons, interview by David Sylvester, in *Jeff Koons, Easyfun—Ethereal* (Berlin: Deutsche Guggenheim, 2001), p. 32.

135: Robert Hughes, review, *Time Magazine*, Feb. 8, 1993.

137: Nan Goldin, interview by Scott Rothkopf, in *Harvard Advocate*, Oct. 1, 2001.

138: Berger, p. 32.

140: Sherrie Levine, quoted in Martha Buskirk and Mignon Nixon, eds., *The Duchamp Effect: Essays, Interviews, Round Table* (Cambridge: MIT Press, 1996), p. 178.

140: Hickey, p. 99.

ADVERTISEMENT AND ART CREDITS

Numbers preceding entries refer to page numbers.

Front cover: Schlitz ad, reprinted courtesy of Pabst Brewing Company.

Back cover: Ikea "Venus on the Half Shell" ad, reprinted courtesy of Carmichael Lynch.

4: ACI ad, private collection.

5: Encompass Insurance ad, featuring Eastman Johnson's *Washington Crossing the Delaware*, ©AR, New York, reprinted courtesy of Leo Burnett, Chicago.

6: Dewar's ad, reprinted courtesy of Leo Burnett, Chicago.

9: Young & Rubicam, Inc. ad, 1945, reprinted courtesy of Young & Rubicam, Inc., New York.

11: Absolut Vodka "Absolut Museum" ad, reprinted courtesy of TBWA Chiat/Day, New York.

15: Pears' Soap "Bubbles" ad, featuring Sir John Everett Millais's *A Child's World*, private collection.

16: Pears' Soap ad, an amalgamation of images from Sir John Everett Millais's *A Child's World* and other paintings and other Pears' ads, private collection.

17: Pears' Soap "Bubbles" ad, private collection.

18: B. T. Babbitt's Soap ad/poster, featuring Sir Edwin Landseer's *The Honeymoon*, private collection, Brooklyn, New York.

19: Ivory Soap ad, featuring J. C. Leyendecker's illustration, private collection.

20: Sungard ads, private collection.

21: Tabu Perfume ads, reprinted courtesy of New Dana Perfumes.

22: Campari ad, created by Steve Campbell (based on Edouard Manet's *The Bar at the Folies-Bergére*), 1980, reprinted courtesy of Campari International and Austin, Nichols & Co., Inc.

23: The St. Regis, New York, ad, reprinted courtesy of Starwood Hotels.

24-25: United Airlines: Chicago/Paris ad, photography by Hunter Freeman (based on George Seurat's *La Grande Jatte*), reprinted courtesy of Hunter Freeman, ©2000 United Airlines, Inc. All Rights Reserved.

28: Levi's ad, featuring Michelangelo's *The David*, ca. 1970, reprinted courtesy of Young & Rubicam, Italy.

29: Bassett-Walker® Apparel Corp. ad, reprinted courtesy of Bassett-Walker® Apparel Corp.

30-31: New York Times ads, featuring artwork by Norman Rockwell: *Freedom from Fear; Schoolteacher in Classroom; Grandfather, Boy, and Dog (Outward Bound)*, reprinted courtesy of Norman Rockwell Family Agency, ©2003 The Norman Rockwell Family Agency and Bozell Worldwide.

32: Volkswagon ad, "Lemon." ©1960 Volkswagon picture, private collection.

33: Mercedes-Benz USA E Class ad campaign, featuring James Abbott McNeill Whistler's *Arrangement in Grey and Black No. 1: The Artist's Mother*, (stock photograph of Whistler's painting by ©Francis G. Mayer/CORBIS; still-life objects by Mark Weiss; car photograph by Tim Damon, Damon Productions, Inc.), reprinted courtesy of Merkley Newman Harty/Partners.

34: Tela ad, reprinted courtesy of Kimberly Schweiz GmbH and Advico Young & Rubicam, Zurich.

The Episcopal Church ad, reprinted courtesy of Fallon McElligott, Minneapolis, 1985.

35: Clear Blue Pregnancy Test ad, reprinted courtesy of Young & Rubicam, São Paulo.

36-37: Nike's Inter-Milan Outdoor ad campaign, illustrators/painters: Dominique Gaucher and Raphael Sottoliloto, 1998, reprinted courtesy of Weiden + Kennedy Amsterdam.

37: ACB+ "The Rapt" ad, reprinted courtesy of Canal+, Spain.

40: Attorney General John Ashcroft at the Justice Department, Washington, D.C., 2001, reprinted courtesy of Associated Press; photographer: Kamenko Pajic.

42-43: Bunte "Cleopatra" ad, reprinted courtesy of Springer & Jacoby, Hamburg.

44: Trio Popular Arts Televison: "Uncensored Month: June," reprinted courtesy of Trio Network, ©2002 Trio Network, Inc.

45: Kellogg's Corn Flakes ad, reprinted courtesy of The Advertising Archive.

46: H2O Plus ad, reprinted courtesy of H2O Plus and P + R Group.

Gyne-moistrin Vaginal Moisturizing Gel ad, reprinted courtesy of Schering-Plough Corporation and Donahue Purhoit Miller.

47: Ikea "Venus on the Half Shell" ad, reprinted courtesy of Carmichael Lynch.

48: The Shell Companies ad, private collection.

49: Textron, Inc. lingerie ad, private collection.

50-51: Maidenform Bra ads., private collection.

52: Robin Bruce furniture ads, reprinted courtesy of AdWorks, Washington, D.C.

53: Rest Assured ads, reprinted courtesy of Joe Public Take-Away Advertising, Capetown, South Africa.

56: Prince Spaghetti Sauce ad, "Original. Chunky," reprinted courtesy of Fallon McElligott, Minneapolis.

57: McDonald's Canada ad, reprinted courtesy of Cossette Communication, Montreal.

58: Marcel Duchamp, *L.H.O.O.Q.*, 1919, Rectified Readymade reproduction of Leonardo da Vinci's *Mona Lisa*, to which Duchamp added mustache, goatee, and title in pencil, 7 3/4 x 4 7/8 in., courtesy of Collection Achim Moeller Fine Art, New York ©Succession Marcel Duchamp, 2003 ARS, New York/ADAGP, Paris.

Leblanc L-70 clarinet ad, reprinted courtesy of G. Leblanc Corporation.

59: Gibson Guitars ad, "Win! Win! Win!," reprinted courtesy of Gibson Musical Instruments.

60: Fujifilm Digital ad, "The Mona Debbie," ©Raphael Fuchs photography, reprinted courtesy of ©Fuji Photo Film USA, Inc.

Cobra Parfums Weil Paris Co. ad, 1945, private collection.

61: Kung Fu Kitchen ad, reprinted courtesy of Barnhart/CMI, Denver.

62: Olin Industries, Inc. "The Gunsmith and the Lady" ad, private collection.

63: Got Milk? ad, reprinted courtesy of Bozell Agency and Iman.
64: Ford Ranger 4 x 4 "Da Vinci Worked in Oils. We prefer Mud" ad, reprinted courtesy of J. Walter Thompson, Detroit.
65: Fiat "Did Leonardo Da Vinci Design the First Fiat?" ad, private collection.
66-67: Sony Handycam ad, reprinted courtesy of Tandem Campmany Guasch, DDB, Barcelona.
70: Marcel Duchamp, *Apolinère Enameled*, 1965, pencil and paint on cardboard and painted tin, 9 5/8 x 13 3/8 in., reprinted courtesy of Collection Achim Moeller Fine Art, New York.
71: Schiaparelli ad, reprinted courtesy of The Advertising Archive.
72: Hanes ad (detail), 1947, private collection.
73: Datsun ad, private collection.
74-75: Grand Marnier "Slightly Less Mysterious" and "To Grand Expectations" ads, 1995, reprinted courtesy of Kirshenbaum Bond & Partners.
75: Paul Delvaux, *The Break of Day*, 1937, oil on canvas, 120 x 150.5 cm. The Solomon R. Guggenheim Foundation, New York, Peggy Guggenheim Collection, Venice.
76: Corday Perfume ad, private collection.
77: Duracell Batteries ad, reprinted courtesy of The Advertising Archive.
78: Koppers Company ads, Illustrations by Bingham, 1943, private collection.
79: Salvador Dali, *The Persistence of Memory*, 1931, oil on canvas, 9 1/2 x 13 in. The Museum of Modern Art, New York, NY, USA. Given anonymously. Digital Image ©The Museum of Modern Art/ Licensed by SCALA/ AR, NY, ©2002 Salvador Dali, Gala-Salvador Dali Foundation/ARS, NY.
Gap Khakis ad, Salvador Dali photograph by Lies Wiegman, reprinted courtesy of Lies Wiegman-Pix Inc./Time Inc. Picture Collection. ©Gap 1994.
Datsun ad, private collection.
80: Bryan's Hosiery ad, private collection.
81: Dettol Ointment ad, reprinted courtesy of The Advertising Archive.
85*: Herbert Bayer, *Destiny of an old Directory*, from the Early series, 1939, gouache and gelatin silver print on paperboard, 18 x 15 9/16 in. Smithsonian American Art Museum, Washington, D.C. USA. Gift of the Container Corporation of America. ©Smithsonian American Art Museum, Washington, D.C. / Art Resource, NY.
87: De Beers Consolidated Mines, Ltd. ads, private collection.
89*: Willem de Kooning, *The Netherlands*, from the United Nations series, 1944, acrylic on prepared fiberboard, 31.9 x 27.4 cm. Smithsonian American Art Museum, Washington, D.C., USA. Gift of the Container Corporation of America. ©Smithsonian American Art Museum, Washington, D.C./Art Resource, NY, USA. ©ARS, NY.
90*: Gyorgy Kepes, *Responsibility*, from the Early series, 1938, gouache and airbrush on paperboard, 20 x 15 in. Smithsonian American Art Museum, Washington, D.C., USA. Gift of the Container Corporation of America. ©Smithsonian American Art Museum, Washington, D.C./Art Resource, NY.
92*: Herbert Bayer, "The things that will destroy America are prosperity at any price, peace at any price, safety first instead of duty first, and love of soft living and the get-rich-quick theory of life." –Theodore Roosevelt, from the Great Ideas of Western Man series, 1959, collage, watercolor, and gouache on paperboard. Smithsonian American Art Museum, Washington, D.C., USA. Gift of the Container Corporation of America. ©Smithsonian American Art Museum, Washington, D.C./Art Resource, NY.
93*: Fernand Léger, *France Reborn*, from the United Nations series, 1945, watercolor, gouache, and pencil on paper, mounted on paperboard, 66.2 x 55.5 cm. Smithsonian American Art Museum, Washington, D.C., USA. Gift of the Container Corporation of America. ©Smithsonian American Art Museum, Washington, D.C./Art Resource, NY. ©ARS, NY.
94*: James Rosenquist, *That margin between . . .*, 1965, oil on canvas, 48 1/8 x 44 1/4 in. Smithsonian American Art Museum, Washington, D.C., USA. Gift of the Container Corporation of America. ©Smithsonian American Art Museum, Washington, D.C./Art Resource, NY. ©VAGA, NY.
95*: René Magritte, "Those who cannot remember the past are condemned to repeat it" – George Santayana, *The Life of Reason*, 1905, from the Great Ideas of Western Man series, ca.1962, gouache and pencil on paper. Smithsonian American Art Museum, Washington, D.C., USA. Gift of the Container Corporation of America. ©Smithsonian American Art Museum, Washington, D.C./Art Resource, NY. ©ARS, NY.
Jacob Lawrence, *Men exist for the sake of one another, Teach them then or bear with them*, from the Great Ideas of Western Man series, 1958, oil on prepared fiberboard, 20 3/4 x 16 3/4 in. Smithsonian American Art Museum, Washington, D.C., USA. Gift of the Container Corporation of America. ©Smithsonian American Art Museum, Washington, D.C./Art Resource, NY.
Henry Moore, from the United Nations series, 1944, ink, watercolor, pencil, crayon, and gouache on paper, 14 15/16 x 11 in. Smithsonian American Art Museum, Washington, D.C., USA. Gift of the Container Corporation of America. ©Smithsonian American Art Museum, Washington, D.C./Art Resource, NY. ©Henry Moore Foundation. Britain.
Joseph Cornell, " Ideals are like stars; you will not succeed in touching them with your hands . . .," from the Great Ideas of Western Man series, ca.1957-58, painted and stained wood, glass shells, etc., 44.2 x 32.7 x 8.9 cm. Smithsonian American Art Museum, Washington, D.C., USA. Gift of the Container Corporation of America. ©Smithsonian American Art Museum, Washington, D.C./Art Resource, NY. ©VAGA, NY.
98: Richard Hamilton, *Just What is It that Makes Today's Homes So Different, So Appealing?*, 1956, collage, 26 x 25 cm. Kunsthalle Tübingen. Collection G. F. Zundel.
99: Andy Warhol, *Campbell's Soup Cans*, 1962, synthetic polymer paint on 32 canvases, each 20 x 16 in. The Museum of Modern Art, New York, NY, USA. Gift of Irving Blum; Nelson A. Rockefeller Bequest, gift of Mr. and Mrs. William A. M. Burden, Abby Aldrich Rockefeller Fund, gift of Nina and Gordon Bunshaft in honor of Henry Moore, Lillie P. Bliss Bequest, Philip Johnson Fund, Frances Keech Bequest, gift of Mrs. Bliss Parkinson, and Florence B. Wesley Bequest (all by exchange). Digital Image ©The Museum of Modern Art/ Licensed by SCALA/AR, NY, ©2002 Andy Warhol Foundation for the Visual Arts.
100: Roy Lichtenstein, *Girl with Ball*, 1961, oil and synthetic polymer paint on canvas, 60 1/4 x 36 1/4 in. The Museum of Modern Art, New York, NY, USA. Gift of Philip Johnson, Digital Image ©The Museum of Modern Art/ Licensed by SCALA/ AR, NY, ©Estate of Roy Lichtenstein.
Mount Airy Lodge ad, ca. 1963, private collection.
102-103: Nivea ad, illustration by Alain Biltereyst, 1999, reprinted courtesy of GV/Company.
104: Philip Morris ad, ca. 1960, private collection.
105: James Rosenquist, *The Light That Won't Fail I*, 1961, oil on canvas, 71 3/4 x 96 1/2 in. Hirshhorn Museum and Sculpture Garden, Smithsonian Institution. Gift of the Joseph H. Hirshhorn Foundation, 1966 (photograph by Lee Stalsworth).
106: Andy Warhol, *Dr. Schol*, 1960, syntheic polymer paint on canvas, 48 x 40 in. The Metropolitan Museum of Art, New York, All Rights Reserved. ©2002 Andy Warhol Foundation for the Visual Arts/ARS, New York.
107: Fred Perry Ltd. ad, "Chaps" (featuring a recycled image from a 1965 trade brochure), 2002, reprinted courtesy of Fred Perry and Avalon Group.
108: Campbell's V/8 ad, reprinted courtesy of Campbell Soup Company.
109: Scoresby Scotch Whisky ad, private collection.
Sunlight ad, ©1987 Lever Brothers Company, private collection.
113-114, 116-117: Absolut Vodka ads (including art by Andy Warhol, Keith Haring, Ed Ruscha, Alonzo Adams, Eugeni Mitta, Kosolapov), reprinted courtesy of TBWA Chiat/Day, New York.
119: Stolichnaya Vodka ad (including art by Eugeni Mitta and Yuri Gorbachev), reprinted courtesy of Margeotes + Fertitta.
120: Imperial Hiram Walker's Blended Whisky ad, painting by Thomas Hart Benton, private collection.
121: Courvoisier Cognac ads, ca. 1970, private collection.
123: Absente Liquor ad, "The Changing Face of Van Gogh" painting by Ron English, 2001, reprinted courtesy of Crillon Importers Ltd. and Gigante Vaz Partners.
127: *Murder by Latitude* paperback cover, private collection.
128: Hans Haacke, *The Right to Life*, 1979, color photograph on three-color silkscreen print, 50 1/4 x 40 1/4 in. Allen Memorial Art Museum, Oberlin College, Oberlin, Ohio. R. T. Miller, Jr. Fund, 1983. ©2002 ARS, New York/VG Bild-Kunst, Bonn.
130: Barbara Kruger, *Untitled (Your Body is a Battleground)*, 1989, photographic silkscreen/vinyl, 112 x 112 in. The Broad Art Foundation, Santa Monica, California, courtesy of Mary Boone Gallery, New York (photograph ©2002 Zindman/Fremont, NYC).
131: Rostov Vodka ad, reprinted courtesy of Lobo Advertising, Minneapolis.
132: Jenny Holzer, *Arno*, 1996, electronic LED sign; blue diodes, 77 x 5 1/4 x 3 in., courtesy of Cheim & Reid, New York.
133: Richard Prince, *Untitled* (Cowboy), 1991/92, Ektacolor photograph, 48 x 72 in., courtesy of Barbara Gladstone.
134: Jeff Koons, *Art Magazine Ads: Banality* (School Children), 1988/89, lithograph, portfolio of 4, 45 x 37 1/4 in., courtesy of Sonnabend Gallery, New York.
135: Jeff Koons, *I Could Go for Something Gordon's*, 1986, courtesy of Sonnabend Gallery, New York.
Jeff Koons, *Stay in Tonight*, 1986, courtesy of Sonnabend Gallery, New York.
136: Jessica Craig-Martin Altoids tin, reprinted courtesy of Jessica Craig-Martin and Hunter Public Relations.
Damien Hirst, Camel cigarette pack, reprinted courtesy of Damien Hirst.
137: Tracey Emin, "Taste. And See." ad for Bombay Blue Sapphire Gin, 1998, reprinted courtesy of Bacardi and Company and Lehmann Maupin.
138: Gavin Turk, *Untitled*, 2002, Xerox digital print, courtesy of private collection.
Xerox ad, reprinted courtesy of Harrison Troughton Wunderman, London.
139: Xerox ad campaign, reprinted courtesy of Young & Rubicam, New York.
George Rodrigue, *PC Blues*, 2001, mixed media on canvas, 60 x 48 inches, courtesy of private collection.
140: Dick Detzner, *Last Pancake Breakfast*, oil on wood, 70 x 36 in. ©2000 Dick Detzner. All rights reseved.
141: The Art Guys, *The Clothes Make the Man*, courtesy of Art Guys, Inc., Worldwide.

***Note:** The original artwork for the Container Corporation of America advertising series featured in this chapter is in the collection of the Smithsonian American Art Museum, Washington, D.C.

SELECTED BIBLIOGRAPHY

The discussion in these chapters owes a great debt to many researchers and critics. For further exploration the following references are invaluable. For the story of Pears' soap and an overview of the subject see Mike Dempsey, ed., *Early Advertising Art from A. & F. Pears Ltd.* (Glasgow: Wm. Collins Sons & Co. Ltd, 1978), James B. Twitchell *Adcult USA, The Triumph of Advertising in American Culture* (New York: Columbia University Press, 1996) and *Twenty Ads That Shook The World* (New York: Three Rivers Press, 2000). A closer reading of the history of art and advertising is found in Wanda M. Corn, *The Great American Thing: Modern Art and National Identity, 1915-1935* (Berkeley: University of California Press, 1999) as well as in Michelle H. Bogart, *Artists, Advertising and the Borders of Art* (Chicago: University of Chicago Press, 1995). For a thorough look at the development of the Container Corporation of America's role see James Sloan Allen, *The Romance of Commerce and Culture* (Chicago: University of Chicago Press, 1983) as well as Neil Harris, ed., *Cultural Excursions* (Chicago: University of Chicago Press, 1990). To get the full force of the debate on pop and other movements, see Steven Henry Madoff, ed., *Pop Art: A Critical History* (Berkeley: University of California Press, 1997), Francis Frascina, ed., *Pollock and After: The Critical Debate Second Edition* (London: Routledge, 2000), Ann Goldstein and Anne Rorimer, *Reconsidering the Object of Art: 1965-1975* (Cambridge, Mass.: The MIT Press, 1996), Lisa Phillips, *The American Century: Art and Culture 1950-2000* (New York: Whitney Museum of American Art, 2000), Kirk Varnadoe and Adam Gopnik, *High and Low: Modern Art and Popular Culture* (New York: Museum of Modern Art, 1990), Thomas Crow, *Modern Art in The Common Culture* (New Haven and London: Yale University Press, 1996), Brandon Taylor, *Avant-Garde and After: Rethinking Art Now* (New York: Harry N. Abrams, 1995), Matthew Collings, *This is Modern Art* (New York: Watson Guptil, 2000), Julian Stallabrass, *High Art Lite, British Art in the 1990s* (New York: Verso, 1999), Raphael Sassower and Louis Cicotello, *The Golden Avant-Garde: Idolatry, Commercialism, and Art* (Charlottesville and London: University of Virginia Press, 2000), and for a clear overview, John Berger, *Ways of Seeing* (London: British Broadcasting Corporation and Penguin Books, 1972). For general cultural and economic observations, Tyler Cowen, *In Praise of Commercial Culture* (Cambridge, Mass: Harvard University Press, 1998), Gary Cross, *An All-Consuming Century: Why Commercialism Won in Modern America* (New York: Columbia University Press, 2000), Alexis De Tocqueville, *Democracy In America*, C.H. Mansfield and D. Winthrop, eds. (Chicago: University of Chicago Press, 2000), and Herbert J. Gans, *Popular Culture and High Culture* (New York: Basic Books, 2000) are essential reading.

For Sam Hoffman, who made selling an art.

Acknowledgments

Like most things associated with advertising, this book was an act of collaboration. My thanks to Leslie Stoker, whose entrepreneurial curiosity about the subject sparked the proposal that became the finished product. My tireless editor, Sandy Gilbert, knows how much her good judgement and high energy made all this possible. David Brown didn't just track down lost ads, haunt libraries and stalk eBay sellers, he also provided an astute sounding board for all matters commercial and aesthetic. Galen Smith's design transformed disparate parts into a cogent whole, while Niloo Tehranchi made sure every detail was perfect. Francine Almash was indefatigable at nailing down permissions, from artists, agencies, companies, and museums around the world. Peg Haller's editorial omniscience made every sentence better, and Jackie Kristel's close readings made sure they stayed that way. Conversations with Dick Detzner, Hans Haacke, George Rodrique, and Gavin Turk offered helpful guidance. For encouragement and ideas both large and small, thanks to Lorrie Bodger, Claudia Deutsch, Arthur Einstein, Jim Ferguson, Belle Frank, Rita Jacobs, Maggie and Michael Malone, Amanda Mecke, Mary Ann Zeman, and my honorary art historian, Dennis Kleinman. For the use of the hall and other comforts, thanks to Victoria Sharp. For sticking in there, no one is better than Roger and Loriann Ho. For love and support beyond the call of duty, special thanks to Jane Weiss.

Text copyright © 2002 Barry Hoffman

All rights reserved. No portion of this book may be reproduced, stored in a retrieval system, or transmitted in any form or by any means, mechanical, electronic, photocopying, recording, or otherwise, without written permission from the publisher.

Published in 2002 by Stewart, Tabori & Chang, A Company of La Martinière Groupe, 115 West 18th Street, New York, NY 10011

Export Sales to all countries except Canada, France, and French-speaking Switzerland: Thames and Hudson Ltd., 181A High Holborn, London WC1V 7QX, England

Canadian Distribution: Canadian Manda Group, One Atlantic Avenue, Suite 105, Toronto, Ontario M6K 3E7, Canada

Library of Congress Cataloging-in-Publication Data
Hoffman, Barry (Barry Howard), 1946-
The fine art of advertising / by Barry Hoffman.
  p. cm.
ISBN 1-58479-222-1
1. Commercial art—United States—History—20th century. I. Title.

NC998.5.A1H64 2003
741.6'7'09730904—dc21

The text of this book was composed in FF DIN.
Edited by Sandra Gilbert
Designed by Galen Smith with Niloo Tehranchi
Graphic Production by Kim Tyner

Printed in Italy

10 9 8 7 6 5 4 3 2 1
First Printing